15 Beginner-Friendly Patterns to
Create Your Vintage-Inspired Closet

Retro Crochet Style

Savannah Price
Creator of Savannah's Stitches

PAGE STREET
PUBLISHING CO.

PAGE STREET
PUBLISHING CO.

First published in 2023 by
Page Street Publishing Co.
27 Congress Street, Suite 1511
Salem, MA 01970
www.pagestreetpublishing.com

Distributed by Macmillan, sales in Canada by The Canadian Manda Group.

27 26 25 24 23   2 3 4 5 6

ISBN-13: 9781645678915
ISBN-10: 1645678911

Library of Congress Control Number: 2022950263

Cover and book design by Emma Hardy for Page Street Publishing Co.
Photography by Savannah Price

Printed and bound in the United States

To my mom, whose selflessness knows no bounds. Thank you for loving me and my work. You're the reason this book exists.

Table of

Contents

Introduction

For as long as I can remember, I've heard the phrase "Start dieting now for the perfect summer body!" repeated at all times of the year. The rise of fast fashion combined with rapidly changing beauty standards often results in clothes that aren't made to fit us; they are cheaply made to flatter whatever body is in style, which is typically not a realistic body at all. We should not be expected to shrink ourselves in order to look "good" —whatever that means. This was a lesson I learned when I started making clothes for myself through crochet.

For most of human history, clothes were tailored to each person's unique body measurements. But now that they aren't, and different stores have vastly different sizing standards, I have had to watch my loved ones lose their confidence as they try on pieces that are created for bodies that most people, genetically, cannot have.

Enter crochet.

Before I discovered crochet, I had vastly underestimated the value of making clothing for your specific measurements. Now I get to put smiles on people's faces with handmade pieces. Not only do my friends and family feel the love I put into every stitch, but they also revel in the fact that nothing has fit them this well before, prompting them to actually embrace their extra curves instead of trying to hide them.

Both my parents are accountants, so while I've gravitated toward different creative pursuits my entire life, I always thought that something more practical was going to be my future. I started crocheting during the summer before my first semester of college and found that it clicked with me like nothing before.

While it is inherently creative, crochet is also incredibly technical. For the first time, I found that as I built stitches and sewed together wonky squares, I could visualize how to make garments that I had always wanted in my wardrobe.

Throughout the next year of my crocheting journey, I found my style. I'm truly Southern born and raised; I lean toward modest clothing with one extra detail to spice it up, like the see-through sleeves on the Daisy Daze Dress (page 71) or the extra texture in the Bucur Sweater (page 97). I also lean toward silhouettes that cinch at your natural waist but give you extra room at other areas of your body.

Thus, while writing this book, I knew what I wanted to create: retro-style patterns that look modern, are easy to make and adjust, even for beginners, and are size-inclusive. While trying to find my style, I bought many vintage patterns that had incredibly limited sizing, so I wanted to do my part to give fiber artists the opportunity to create vintage-inspired garments with ease.

For the six months that I wrote this book, I used my lovely friends and fellow college students as models to don designs inspired by my love of florals, fun colors and the beauty of my home state of Kentucky. Now, those designs are yours to make, love and cherish, as all handmade garments should be.

All bodies are beautiful, and we all deserve beautiful clothes to adorn ourselves. I hope this book can become a useful part of your crochet journey.

Savannah

How to Use This Book

All of the patterns in this book are beginner friendly. If you know a few basic stitches (ch, sc, dc), it will be easy for you to learn how to create these designs, with a couple unique techniques thrown into each pattern.

The first section, A Beginner's Guide to Crocheting Garments (page 9), is meant for folks who have never made a garment before, and may be completely new to reading written patterns. It has general tips and information that can be applied to most crochet patterns that are up to industry standard.

The last section, Crochet Techniques (page 135), includes crochet methods that are specific to the patterns in this book that even those who have crocheted a garment before may not know.

For more images of the designs, you can scroll through my Instagram @savannah.stitches. I also offer pattern support—email me anytime at sspstitches@gmail.com.

I'm so excited for you to create your handmade vintage-inspired wardrobe. Let's dive in!

A Beginner's Guide to Crocheting Garments

READING PATTERNS

It can seem difficult to understand the abbreviations, stitch counts and garment sizing when you are first learning how to read patterns, but you'll quickly get the hang of it. Unless otherwise indicated, the following notes apply to all patterns.

Seaming

When seaming pieces together, make sure to keep seams loose and do not pull tight so that pieces are able to stretch; otherwise, tight seams will affect the fit and restrict your movement while wearing them.

Turning Chains

When starting a row with single crochet, the ch-1 turning chain **does not** count as a stitch. When starting a row with double crochet, the ch-2 turning chain **does** count as a stitch. In photo A, the hook is pointing to where you will create your first double crochet; photo B shows what it will look like after you've completed your first double crochet and now have two stitches.

Stitch Counts

Stitch counts are listed after each row or round. If no stitch count is given, there has been no change since the previous row/round.

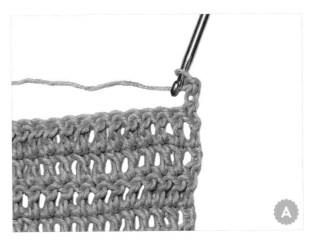

Sizing

Remember that you're only following the numbers that apply to your size, so the instructions are usually less overwhelming than they look. If it helps, you can circle the numbers that pertain to your size or leave a sticky note next to each one.

In this book, most patterns have nine sizes ranging from sizes XS–5XL. A few have merged two or three sizes together while covering the same size range. Instructions on how to read the parentheses are available in each pattern. For garments with 9 sizes, they are typically written as follows: Size 1 (2, 3, 4, 5) (6, 7, 8, 9), which correspond to the Craft Yarn Council sizes of XS (S, M, L, XL) (2X, 3X, 4X, 5X). For garments with 5 sizes, they are typically written as follows: Size 1 (2, 3, 4, 5) which correspond to the Craft Yarn Council sizes of XS (M, XL, 3X, 5X).

When you're reading the pattern, you will only follow the numbers that pertain to the size you choose. For example, here's a line from the Daisy Daze Dress:

* With your base color yarn, ch 63 (66, 74, 81, 88) (95, 103, 110, 119).

* This means that for size 1, you will chain 63; for size 2, you will chain 66; for size 3, you will chain 74; and so on. The two sets of parentheses make it easier to find your size. For example; if you follow size 5, you'll always look at the last number in the first set of parentheses. Once you know where your size is, it'll become easier to find it every time.

U.S. (a.k.a. Imperial) and metric measurements will always be provided, with U.S. written first, followed by the corresponding metric units.

When asterisks surround a set of instructions, it indicates that the instructions should be repeated as many times as indicated.

For example, here's a line from the Sunbeam Skirt:

* Ch 3, then *tc 16 (18, 21, 23, 26) (28, 31, 33, 35), inc; repeat from * to end of row.

* When you see the asterisk, you work the instructions following the asterisk the first time you read it. This means that for size 1, you will chain 3, triple crochet in the next 16 stitches, then increase on the 17th. Now, repeat the set of instructions after the asterisk until the end of the row or as directed.

Another way that repeated instructions can be written is with brackets. When brackets surround a series of stitches, they will always be followed by the total number of times the bracketed stitches should be worked, or instructions like "to end of row." For example: In the griddle stitch, we alternate working sc and dc stitches along the entire row. This is written as:

* Sc in first st, dc in next st, [sc in next st, dc in next st] to end of row.

* After working the first 2 stitches, we will work 1 sc in next st, then 1 dc in next st, then 1 sc in next st, then 1 dc in next st and on and on until we've worked all stitches in the row.

When parentheses surround a set of instructions, it indicates that the sequence inside the parentheses should be worked into the same stitch/space. For example, here's a line from the Starburst Granny Square:

* (dc4tog, ch 2) into each ch-1 sp around.

* This means that into each chain-1 space, you will work a double crochet 4 together, then chain 2 before moving onto the next chain-1 space.

Abbreviations in US Crochet Terms

 * blo: back loops only

 * ch: chain

 * dc: double crochet

 * dc2tog: double crochet two together

 * fpdc: front post double crochet

 * sc: single crochet

 * st/sts: stitch/stitches

 * yo: yarn over

All of the stitches and methods used in this book are basic, beginner-friendly stitches with explanations for less common things, such as the puff stitch or how to crochet in the back loops only, which you'll find in the Techniques section (page 135). If after reading the explanations for stitches you are still unsure on how to do it, I recommend looking up a beginner's tutorial for that stitch on YouTube—there is a plethora of beginner crochet tutorials online.

MATERIALS

Choosing the Right Yarn

The yarn that I used to create the patterns in this book vary greatly from brand to brand, but you never have to use that exact yarn; it can become very pricey very quickly, and you don't need to use expensive yarn to have an expensive-looking result. I would recommend using the same yarn weight that I do, but you can easily change the fiber content and brand to fit your preferences.

 * **Weight:** All the patterns in this book use the same yarn weight. It's known by many different names, but it's most often called "size 4," "aran," "worsted" or "afghan." If the yarn you want to use doesn't have any of those labels, you simply have to check if it meets gauge; if it does, then it's okay to use!

 * **Fiber content:** You don't have to use the same fiber (wool, cotton, acrylic, etc.) that I used in the patterns, but it may affect the performance of your garment. For example, cotton is a heavy fiber, so if you replace the recommended acrylic with cotton, it may sag more than expected with the extra weight.

 * **Dye lots:** When you start a garment pattern, you'll be using a lot of yarn, and thus probably more than one skein. Because of this, you'll need to check the dye lots on your skeins before starting. Even if two skeins are labeled as the same color, they can look very different if they come from different dye lots, and the difference will become apparent once you start crocheting with them. Ensure that you have the same dye lot for each skein before you begin. You will find this on the label of the yarn.

Crochet Hook

Each pattern in this book recommends a US H/8 (5 mm) hook, but if your gauge swatch shows you should use a smaller or larger hook, you may want to have those purchased and at the ready. It can become expensive to buy each hook as you go, so I would recommend buying a set. If you have issues with wrist, arm or shoulder pain, you can use ergonomic hooks.

Notions

* **Tape measure:** Getting a tape measure is essential to fiber artistry. I would recommend getting a soft tape measure made specifically for clothing. Make sure yours is approximately 60 inches (152 cm) long, but if you're often making larger sizes, you can get a larger tape measure.

* **Tapestry needle:** Also known as a yarn needle or darning needle, this is another essential for fiber artistry. It is mainly used for sewing different pattern pieces together and weaving in ends. Since all pieces in this book will require seaming, this is an investment you want to make. Plastic and metal needles are available, but with much use, plastic can bend and break. I recommend buying a good metal needle, or two!

* **Stitch markers:** Locking stitch markers are used in most patterns in this book. They are very useful for aligning and securing panels for seaming and marking stitch placements. There is no need to buy some if you don't want to; scrap pieces of yarn, safety pins or anything else that you can tie or lock onto a stitch will work just fine. If you do buy some, though, make sure to get a lot, since they go missing often! An inexpensive set is just as functional and good as an expensive set.

MEASUREMENTS

How to Choose a Size

This book follows the Craft Yarn Council's sizing standards, and the nine sizes correspond to sizes XS–5XL. In this book, the sizes are labeled as 1 through 9 to encourage crocheters to look beyond what size category they typically fall under; as we all know, department stores are notoriously bad about sizing, so you are encouraged to measure yourself and choose a size based on the pattern's recommendations, not on what size you typically fall under.

Each pattern in this book is accompanied by a sizing chart that details the measurements as well as the intended ease for the pattern. Ease is the difference between the size of a finished garment and the size of your body. For example, if your hip circumference is 42 inches (107 cm), and the garment has a finished hip circumference of 45 inches (114 cm), the garment has 3 inches (7 cm) of positive ease, since it measures 3 inches (7 cm) larger than your actual hip circumference. Garments can also have negative ease, which means it measures smaller than your body for a tight-fitting look, but there are no garments with negative ease in this book.

To choose a size, you'll first need to measure yourself. For a sweater, for example, you'll need to know your chest circumference and upper arm circumference. Of course, measurements will differ between people in the same size bracket, so that's why it's important to measure. You can take a hundred people who all fall under the size "medium," and they will all have slightly different measurements because we all naturally distribute our weight differently with our different proportions. This is what's so great about making your own clothes: You can tailor them to suit your measurements in a way that department store clothes could never do.

Each pattern in this book includes a Customized Sizing section to help you adjust the pattern if your measurements don't line up exactly with those provided in the sizing chart. Following the pattern exactly will likely yield a great-fitting garment regardless, but the tips included along the way will allow you to alter the pattern if you feel you need any adjustments for an even better fit.

To choose a size, take your measurements and refer to the ease instructions and model reference to understand what size is best for you.

How to Correctly Measure Yourself

To get the most accurate measurement, make sure your tape measure is held taut against your body. The tape shouldn't be held slack, but it shouldn't be so tight that it's pressing into your skin—just tight enough to mold to the area of the body you're measuring. If you plan on wearing undergarments, such as a bra, tank top, shorts, etc., make sure you measure yourself while wearing those.

* When measuring the upper arm, hold the measuring tape around the circumference of the widest part of your bicep.

* When measuring your chest, hold the measuring tape around the circumference of the widest part of your chest. Make sure the tape is held horizontally all the way around your chest and it doesn't ride up toward your shoulders or down toward your waist. If it does, your measurements will be incorrect.

* When measuring the waist, hold the measuring tape around the circumference of the smallest part of your waist, usually around or above your belly button.

* When measuring the hips, hold the measuring tape around the circumference of the widest part of your hips. Make sure the tape is held horizontally all the way around your hips and the tape doesn't ride up toward your stomach or back, or down toward your thighs.

* When measuring the thighs, hold the measuring tape around the circumference of the widest part of one thigh. This is typically an inch or two below the crotch.

GAUGE SWATCHES

What Is a Gauge Swatch?

Checking your gauge, also known as your tension, is arguably the most important step in making any garment. The gauge swatch is a small sample piece of crocheted fabric you create using the same yarn, hook and stitches you will use for the pattern. Checking your gauge will tell you if your tension is the same as the designer's; if your tension is too loose or too tight, the garment you create can thus be too loose or too tight.

To understand this further, let's look at the gauge in the following photos:

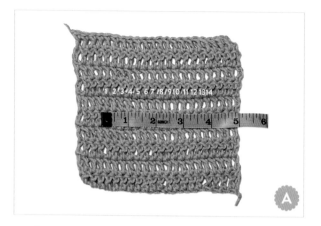

✳ 4 x 4" (10 x 10 cm) = 14.5 sts and 7 rows in double crochet

This means that when you create 14.5 double crochet stitches for 7 rows, you will create a piece of fabric that measures 4 inches (10 cm) wide by 4 inches (10 cm) tall. I recommend creating a gauge swatch that is larger than needed so you aren't measuring the stitches on the edge, which can measure differently than the inner stitches. In practice, for this gauge swatch, you should create 20 to 25 stitches and 10 rows, and measure the inner 14.5 stitches (as seen in photo A) and 7 rows (as seen in photo B).

If you plan to block your finished garment (page 146), make sure you block your gauge swatch as well. Note that blocking is not required, and I typically do not block my garments.

What Happens If My Gauge Is Off?

Every crocheter's gauge is different because of how they hold their yarn and hook, and thus the size of stitches may vary greatly from crocheter to crocheter. Two people can make the same pattern using the same yarn and hook, but if they don't have the same gauge, the finished product will be two completely different sizes.

For example, let's say you're creating size 5 of the Letterman Sweater. The total number of stitches in the chest for your size is 200, intended to make a 52-inch (132-cm) finished chest measurement. If the gauge for this sweater states that there are 10 stitches for every 2.6 inches (7 cm), but your gauge swatch has 12 stitches for every 2.6 inches (7 cm), there are too many stitches in the same space; the stitches are smaller than intended. This means your tension is too tight, and smaller stitches means the sweater will be smaller than intended. In this example, your sweater would end up measuring 43 inches (109 cm) with that gauge, which is two sizes too small. The 2 stitches extra in the gauge swatch may not seem like much of a difference, but it can heavily affect the fit of your finished garment.

To change your tension, you'll need to change your hook size, or try crocheting a little looser or tighter by holding your yarn looser or tighter. Always use the recommended hook size to start. If your tension is tight (too many stitches in the same space), go up one or two hook sizes. If your tension is too loose (too few stitches in the same space), go down one or two hook sizes. It can be a tedious guess-and-check method, but it'll be worth it in the end!

TAKING CARE OF YOUR FINISHED GARMENTS

To keep handmade garments in good condition, they'll need a little extra care. To clean them, handwash them in lukewarm water with mild, gentle detergent or wool wash, then roll in a towel to remove the excess water and lay flat to dry.

Some yarns are machine washable and dryable, including most cottons, acrylics and superwash yarns. Don't assume that your garment is, though! Always check the label on your yarn for specific care instructions. If you machine-wash a garment made of wool, which is hand-washable only, felting will occur.

To store your finished garments, do not hang them up. Unfortunately, the forces of gravity can permanently stretch your garment and ruin the shape, since handmade garments can sometimes be heavy. To avoid this, simply fold your finished garments.

A Day at the Park

With every passing year, the 90-degree days of summer extend longer and longer. While I've grown to love the sun's rays, it's hard to find handmade garments that help you cool down instead of heat up. In these patterns, the combination of cotton yarn and construction methods gives you room to breathe and ensures that you'll be able to achieve the ultimate goal: looking your best in the summer without sweating up a storm.

Intended to be made with bright colors for summer days or earth tones to blend in with the nature around you, these patterns are endlessly customizable. Layer the Gardenia Vest (page 31) over your favorite top to match the plant life around you, or don the Spring Fling Shorts (page 39) to stay stylish while you're active. Explore the infinite possibilities of crocheted skirts with the patchwork Ophelia Skirt (page 47) or the breezy Sunbeam Skirt (page 27). If you want a garment that is perfect for both a full day at a festival or stretching out in the sun, the Floweralls (page 19) have got you covered.

Inspired by the beauty of the flora in my home state of Kentucky, each piece is made with simple patterns and creative techniques that echo summer blooms and natural motifs. When you wear them to your next picnic or outdoor concert, you'll be sure to receive compliments on the clothes you made with your own hands. You're bound to look stylish in the summer heat with these standout staples.

Floweralls

Made for frolics through fields and summer heat, the Floweralls are perfect for days in the sunshine. This pattern combines classic overalls and patchwork with modern, fun colors and standout flowers. Since the Floweralls are made of squares, you'll be able to make progress every time you have 20 minutes to spare. You can make your own piece out of a million colors or just four; it's a choose-your-own adventure for the crocheter. The finishing details of scalloped hems and fun buttons ensure that the Floweralls will pair well with any fun and funky pieces you've been waiting to wear. Layer your Floweralls with a simple T-shirt for the perfect outfit to wear while lying in the grass, or a turtleneck and tights for a chillier day in the shade.

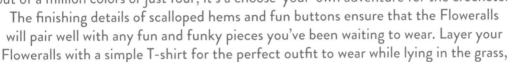

MATERIALS

Yarn

Worsted weight/size 4 yarn in 4 colors, 650–1285 total yds (595–1176 m). See specific yardage amounts for each size in the pattern's size chart on page 20.

Shown In

Modeled: Wool and the Gang Shiny Happy Cotton in the following colors:

* Color 1: Ivory White
* Color 2: Purple Haze
* Color 3: Eucalyptus Green
* Color 4: Mellow Mauve

Step-by-Step: Red Heart Super Saver Yarn in the following colors:

* Color 1: Buff
* Color 2: Soft White
* Color 3: Light Raspberry
* Color 4: Burgundy

Hook

US H/8 (5 mm) or size needed to obtain gauge

Notions

2 buttons (1.5" [4 cm] each)

Tapestry needle

Scissors

Stitch markers

Gauge

4 x 4" (10 x 10 cm) = 15 sts and 7.5 rows in double crochet

For swatch

Ch 21.

Row 1: Dc in 3rd st from hook (skipped sts count as dc) and in each st across, turn. [20 dc]

Rows 2–10: Ch 2 (counts as first dc), dc in each st across, turn.

Block your swatch (page 146) if you plan on blocking your garment. Measure the inner 4 inches (10 cm) of your blocked swatch to get the most accurate measurement.

Floweralls Sizing Chart

	Size 1	Size 2	Size 3	Size 4	Size 5	Size 6	Size 7	Size 8	Size 9
Finished waist measurement	25" 64 cm	30" 76 cm	35" 89 cm	40" 102 cm	45" 114 cm	50" 127 cm	55" 140 cm	60" 152 cm	65" 165 cm
Finished hip measurement	30" 76 cm	35" 89 cm	40" 102 cm	45" 114 cm	50" 127 cm	55" 140 cm	60" 152 cm	65" 165 cm	70" 178 cm
Finished thigh measurement	20" 51 cm	20" 51 cm	25" 64 cm	25" 64 cm	30" 76 cm	30" 76 cm	35" 89 cm	35" 89 cm	40" 102 cm
Yardage required (Color 1, Color 2, Color 3, Color 4)	60, 105, 165, 320	65, 115, 175, 340	75, 130, 205, 380	80, 140, 220, 395	90, 160, 245, 485	95, 170, 260, 505	115, 185, 290, 540	120, 195, 305, 560	130, 215, 330, 610
Total yardage required	650	695	790	835	980	1030	1130	1180	1285
Meters required (Color 1, Color 2, Color 3, Color 4)	55, 96, 151, 293	60, 106, 160, 311	69, 119, 188, 348	74, 128, 202, 362	83, 147, 224, 444	87, 156, 238, 462	106, 170, 266, 494	110, 179, 279, 512	119, 197, 302, 558
Total meters required	595	637	724	766	898	943	1036	1080	1176
Number of squares	23	25	29	31	35	37	41	43	47

This chart shows the finished garment measurements. The Floweralls are meant to be slightly larger or fitted to your waist, hip and thigh measurements. For reference, the model is 5 feet, 4 inches (163 cm) tall with a 27-inch (69-cm) waist, 36-inch (91-cm) hip and 22-inch (56-cm) thigh measurements, and is wearing a size 2 with customized sizing to add one square to each finished thigh (25 inches [64 cm] finished garment measurement) and to add 1 inch (2.5 cm) to the hips. Refer to Customized Sizing (page 21) to do the same. If between sizes, size up. Pattern sizes are written as 1 (2, 3, 4, 5) (6, 7, 8, 9). These sizes align with XS–5XL in the United States.

Customized Sizing

The basic construction of the Floweralls is made of five components: The bib (the square made of 4 squares), the ring of squares that make up the waist, the ring of squares that make up the hips (which is generally one square larger than the waist) and the two rings of squares that make up the thighs. If your measurements do not quite align with the standard sizing, you can make a custom-fit garment by following these steps.

First, take your waist, hip and thigh measurements and round up to the nearest multiple of 5 for inches or 13 for centimeters. For example, a 37-inch (94-cm) waist, 38-inch (97-cm) hip and 24-inch (61-cm) thigh would become a 40-inch (104-cm) waist, 40-inch (104-cm) hip and 25-inch (65-cm) thigh.

Next, divide each of these numbers by either 5 for inches or 13 for centimeters. These numbers would become 8 waist, 8 hip and 5 thigh for both measurements. This is the number of squares needed for each section.

Finally, add up the three numbers (2x the thigh measurement, since there are two legs). Then, add 4 squares for the bib. In the example, we'd now have 30. This is the amount of squares you're going to make.

You'll follow the same construction pattern, adjusting each section to your specific ring sizes. You can also adjust ring sizes by crocheting the desired amount. See Adding Length to Rows of Squares (page 136) for more details.

Base Square

The recommended square is the Starburst Granny Square (page 144), which is used in the sample. You can use any square you like that measures 5 x 5 inches (13 x 13 cm). Refer to the sizing section to see how many squares you should make in total, and complete that many. This is the longest step, but you can do it!

Beginning Assembly

Use a whip stitch (page 135) for all seaming. Remember to always sew pieces together with the wrong sides facing out. I used color 4 for all seaming. Let's look at how we put it all together!

Thighs (make two)

Stitch together 4 (4, 5, 5, 6) (6, 7, 7, 8) squares to create a long row.

Bib

The bib is made of 4 squares in a 2 x 2 panel (photo A). This is the same for all sizes. If you feel like this 10 x 10–inch (25 x 25–cm) panel doesn't give you enough coverage, feel free to double crochet in each stitch around the bib for as many rounds as needed. If you do this, put (2 dc, ch 2, 2 dc) in each outer corner and 2 dc in each ch-sp in the middle of the edges.

Waist

Stitch together 5 (6, 7, 8, 9) (10, 11, 12, 13) squares into a long row.

Hips

Stitch together 6 (7, 8, 9, 10) (11, 12, 13, 14) squares into a long row.

Body Assembly

Stitch your waist and hip rows together using the Whip Stitch Method (page 137), as seen in photo B.

Join together the short ends of these rows to form a ring. The seam you just created will be the front center of your Floweralls. This is your body ring.

Next, stitch together a thigh strip to form a ring. Repeat for the second thigh.

Now we will stitch the crotch area. Align the thigh rings and stitch them together on the edge of the top across one full square. One square should be long enough for most sizes. Only stitch the top of the squares together. This process is shown below in photo C. If you want the crotch area to be shorter, only stitch together half a square. If you want it to be longer, stitch together half of another square.

Next, lay your body ring flat and put a stitch marker into the front center of your overalls at the bottom. Then, put another stitch marker parallel to this one on the back side of the body, as seen in photo D. There should be an equal amount of distance between the two stitch markers; for example, if the bottom of my body ring was 10 squares wide, there would be 5 squares in between each stitch marker.

Next, line up your attached legs under your body ring, putting the crotch where the stitch markers are (photo E). You will not sew the crotch into anything; instead, you will match the next unused stitch on the leg just in front or behind the crotch to the corresponding stitch marker. Stitch together the legs, one at a time, to the body, starting from one stitch marker until you reach the other (photos F and G). If the squares in the thigh ring and body ring do not match up exactly, you may need to apply the Whip Stitch Method (page 137).

Final Details

After you've finished attaching both legs, you will add an edging to the top and bottom of the body. With color 4, join in any stitch on the top of the body ring.

Rounds 1–2: Ch 1, sc in each st around, slst to first st to join (do not turn).

Round 3: Ch 3 (counts as first tc), tc in each sc around, slst to first st to join (do not turn).

Round 4: Ch 1, sc in each tc around, slst to first st to join. Fasten off.

With color 4, join in any st on the lower thighs.

Round 1: Ch 1, sc into each st of thigh, slst to first st to join. Fasten off or work scallop stitch (page 142). Repeat on other leg.

Attaching the Bib

With your work so far laid flat, align the bib so the middle vertical seam lines up with your front center seam and crotch. Using whipstitch (page 135), stitch the bib to the front of your Floweralls.

Work 1 round of sc all the way around the body and on the three external edges of the bib. This round will act as a fifth round atop the waist edging and a first round of bib edging. To get a cleaner finish, sc3tog on the corners attached to the body (bottom left and right of the bib), and sc 3 into upper corners not attached to the body (top left and right of the bib).

Straps (make two)

To figure out the length of straps you need, try on the Floweralls and measure from the back of your waist to over your shoulder, where the bib is. With this measurement, ch 3 for every 1 inch (2.5 cm) using color 4. For example, if your measurement is 20 inches (51 cm), then chain 60.

Chain to calculated length.

Dc in 4th ch from hook (skipped ch-3 counts as a dc), dc in each ch across.

Ch 2 and slst into last ch (photo H).

Ch 2 and turn your work so the row of dc is upside down. Work 1 dc into space between each dc across, as seen in photo I. You won't be working into the ch itself, but instead between the stitches of the dc you just made.

Ch 2 and slst into bottom of skipped ch-3 at beginning.

Ch 2 and slst into top of first dc (photo J). Fasten off. Repeat for the second strap.

Try on your Floweralls to figure out where you'd like to place the straps on the back, and seam them on there as seen in photo K. If you want the straps to cross in the back, I recommend setting them wider apart than if not crossing.

Optional Scallop Edges

Using color 4, complete the scallop stitch (page 142) around the bottom of the legs, all around the body around the bottom of the legs and all around the body (including the sides and top of the bib). You can crochet over any loose ends to avoid having to weave them in.

Note: If you have a difference of more than 1–2 inches (2–5 cm) between your waist measurement and the garment waist measurement, the scallop stitch may become distorted after tying the waist belt. To avoid this, skip 2 stitches instead of 1 during the scallop stitch when crocheting around the waist. You can follow as described for the thighs and bib without distortion.

Creating the Waist Belt

To create the waist chain that you'll use as a belt, first figure out how long you want it to be. I recommend adding 5–10 inches (13–25 cm) to your own waist measurement.

Using color 4, ch 5 for every inch or ch 2 for every cm. For example, for a 40-inch (102-cm) belt, ch 200. Slst into every ch, then fasten off. Weave in the ends.

To use the belt, start from the middle front of the Floweralls in the row of triple crochet. Weave the belt in and out between each tc, all the way around, and tie in the front; you'll be going over and under the posts of tc, as seen in photos L and M.

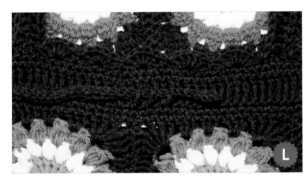

Final Steps

Sew buttons onto the free end of each of your straps with yarn or thread, as seen in photo N. To use the straps, insert the button into the ch-2 gap on each upper corner of the bib, like in photo O.

Weave in any loose ends you may still have—and congratulations! You're finished!

Sunbeam Skirt

Inspired by the flow of summer winds, the Sunbeam Skirt is unique for its breezy structure that allows for movement in a way that few other crochet garments do. The use of triple crochets and a fairly loose gauge combine to create a comfortable skirt that can cinch in at the waist to your liking. The nature of its construction—top-down, in the round—means that you can adjust the length even after finishing the skirt, making it truly customizable and easy to adjust for any occasion. You can make it in alternating bright colors to mimic its namesake, or muted tones for the changing seasons. Wear it with a fun crop top when the sun is beaming or pair it with a chunky sweater and thick tights when the temperatures drop. The Sunbeam Skirt is a versatile closet staple that any crocheter can cherish in their wardrobe.

MATERIALS

Yarn

Worsted weight/size 4 yarn in 2–6 colors (sample was done with 5 colors), 310–1535 total yds (284–1404 m). See specific yardage amounts for each size in the pattern's size chart on page 28.

Shown In

Wool and the Gang Shiny Happy Cotton in the following colors:

* ✳ Color 1: Lilac Wash
* ✳ Color 2: Ivory White
* ✳ Color 3: Duck Egg Blue
* ✳ Color 4: Cameo Rose
* ✳ Color 5: Purple Haze

Hook

US H/8 (5 mm) or size needed to obtain gauge

Notions

Tapestry needle

Scissors

Stitch markers

Gauge

4 x 4" (10 x 10 cm) = 14.5 sts and 4 rows in triple crochet

For swatch

Ch 22.

Row 1: Tc in 4th st from hook (skipped sts count as tc) and in each st across, turn. [20 tc]

Row 2–6: Ch 3 (counts as first tc), tc in each st across, turn.

Block your swatch (page 146) if you plan on blocking your garment. Measure the inner 4 inches (10 cm) of your blocked swatch to get the most accurate measurement. If you aren't getting the right height on your stitches and your rows are too small, you can extend the height of your stitch by lifting the hook more than you usually would as you complete yarn overs and pull throughs.

Sunbeam Skirt Sizing Chart

	Size 1	Size 2	Size 3	Size 4	Size 5	Size 6	Size 7	Size 8	Size 9
Finished waist measurement	28" 71 cm	32" 81 cm	36" 91 cm	40" 102 cm	44" 112 cm	48" 122 cm	52" 132 cm	56" 142 cm	60" 152 cm
Finished hip measurement	33" 84 cm	37" 94 cm	41" 104 cm	45" 114 cm	49" 124 cm	53" 135 cm	57" 145 cm	61" 155 cm	65" 165 cm
Finished skirt length	14" 36 cm	15" 38 cm	16" 41 cm	18" 46 cm	20" 51 cm	22" 56 cm	23" 58 cm	25" 64 cm	26" 66 cm
Total yardage required	310	410	500	700	890	1055	1190	1390	1535
Total meters required	284	375	457	640	814	965	1088	1271	1404

This chart shows the finished garment measurements. This skirt is designed to be worn with anywhere from 2–6 inches (5–15 cm) of positive ease, depending on the size you are making. For reference, the model is 5 feet, 4 inches (163 cm) tall with a 27-inch (69-cm) waist and 36-inch (91-cm) hip measurements, and is wearing a size 2 with 5 inches (13 cm) of positive ease. If between sizes, size up, or refer to Customized Sizing to get the perfect fit. Pattern sizes are written as 1 (2, 3, 4, 5) (6, 7, 8, 9). These sizes align with XS–5XL in the United States.

Customized Sizing

This skirt is made top-down, which means that your initial ch decides how large the waist will be. If you'd like to make the waist slightly smaller or larger, simply adjust your initial starting ch according to gauge. For example, if you want to add 2 inches (5 cm) to your waist measurement, you'd need to add an extra 7 or 8 tc.

If you want to change the hip measurement, that will depend on your waist measurement, since the wider hips are achieved through making increases in each round. There are 18 increases total from the waist to the hips (worked over the first 5 rounds) for all sizes to create a 5-inch (13-cm) increase; then there are four increases in each round after for a 1-inch (2.5-cm) increase per round. To create a larger hip measurement, create more increases along the rounds; to create a smaller hip measurement, exclude increases.

If you want to change the length, you can simply subtract or add rows as you're working.

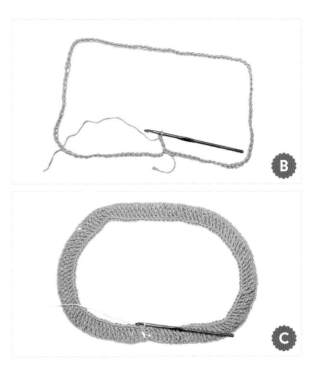

B

Beginning the Skirt

Foundation chain: To start, ch 102 (116, 131, 145, 160) (174, 189, 204, 218). Then, slst into your first ch to join into a circle, as seen in photo A. Make sure you don't twist your chain!

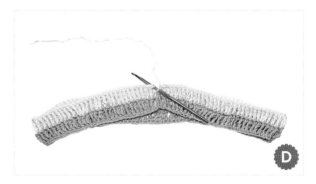

C

Round 2: Ch 3, then [tc in next 15 (17, 20, 22, 25) (27, 30, 32, 34) sts, inc in next st] 6 times, tc in any remaining sts to end, slst into top of ch-3 as seen in photo D. You should now have 108 (122, 137, 151, 166) (180, 195, 210, 224) sts.

A

Round 1: Ch 3 (counts as first tc here and throughout; photo B), tc in each ch around, slst into top of your initial ch-3. You should now have 102 (116, 131, 145, 160) (174, 189, 204, 218) sts.

Tip: To change colors between each round, slst into the ch-3 with your new color as seen in photo C, then carry on as normal.

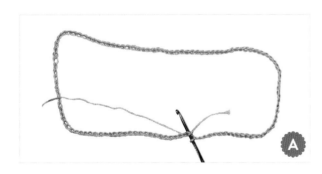

D

Round 3: Ch 3, [tc in next 25 (29, 33, 36, 40) (43, 47, 51, 54) sts, inc in next st] 4 times, tc in any remaining sts to end, slst into top of ch-3. Place a stitch marker in the 2nd tc of each inc. You should have four stitch markers, as seen in photo E. You should now have 112 (126, 141, 155, 170) (184, 199, 214, 228) sts.

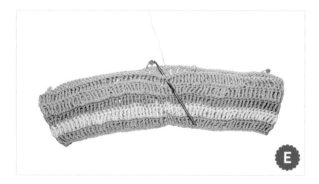

Round 4: Ch 3, then [tc to marked st, inc in that st, move marker up into 2nd st of inc (as seen in photos F and G)] around, tc in each st to end, slst into the top of your ch-3.

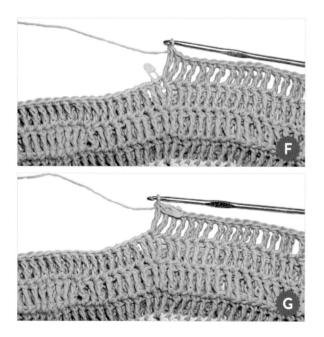

Repeat round 4 for a total of 14 (16, 17, 19, 21) (23, 24, 26, 27) rounds (including the first 4 rounds), moving the stitch marker up each time into the new round. Fasten off, and most of the work is done!

Final Details

Attach your yarn at any point to the top of your skirt (your foundation chain), then ch 1 and sc around. Slst into your first sc, then fasten off for a nice, clean finish.

To create the waist chain that you'll use as a belt, first figure out how long you want it to be. I recommend adding 5–10 inches (12–25 cm) to your own waist measurement.

Using the same color you used for row 1, ch 5 for every inch, or ch 2 for every cm; for example, for a 40-inch (102-cm) belt, ch 200. Slst into every chain, then fasten off. Weave in the ends.

To use the belt, start from any point in row 1. Weave the belt under a tc, then over the top of the next tc, then under the next, as seen in photo H. Repeat this all the way around until you finish, then tie.

Weave in all ends, and congratulations! You're finished!

Gardenia Vest

Create your own wearable garden with the Gardenia Vest. With a simple construction and floral finishes across the front and back, this piece is perfect for beginners looking to expand their knowledge as well as experienced crocheters aiming to perfect their skills. The three body panels make for a simple, lightweight design that complements any outfit. The slip stitch detailing makes sturdy stems that can grow in any direction you choose. The small flower appliques can bloom into dozens of complementary colors or create a sense of unity when made in the same color; the choice is yours! Wear the Gardenia Vest over a crop top or long-sleeve button-up for a simple and sophisticated outfit.

MATERIALS

Yarn

Worsted weight/size 4 yarn in 3–8 colors, 415–1425 total yds (379–1304 m). See specific yardage amounts for each size in the pattern's size chart on page 33.

Shown In

Wool and the Gang Shiny Happy Cotton in the following colors:

 * Color 1: Timberwolf
 * Color 2: Eucalyptus Green

Scrap yarn for flowers: Chalk Yellow, Ivory White, Purple Haze, Lilac Wash, Cameo Rose

Hook

US H/8 (5 mm) or size needed to obtain gauge

Notions

Tapestry needle

Scissors

Stitch markers

Gauge

4 x 4" (10 x 10 cm) = 15.5 sts and 8 rows in double crochet

For swatch:

Ch 21.

Row 1: Dc in 3rd st from hook (skipped sts count as dc) and in each st across, turn. [20 dc]

Row 2–10: Ch 2 (counts as first dc), dc in each st across, turn.

Block your swatch (page 146) if you plan on blocking your garment. Measure the inner 4 inches (10 cm) of your blocked swatch to get the most accurate measurement.

Gardenia Vest Sizing Chart

	Size 1	Size 2	Size 3	Size 4	Size 5	Size 6	Size 7	Size 8	Size 9
Finished waist circumference	28" 71 cm	32" 81 cm	36" 91 cm	40" 102 cm	44" 112 cm	48" 122 cm	52" 132 cm	56" 142 cm	60" 152 cm
Finished armhole gap	12" 30 cm	14" 36 cm	14" 36 cm	16" 41 cm	18" 46 cm	20" 51 cm	22" 56 cm	24" 61 cm	24" 61 cm
Shoulder to hem measurement	15" 38 cm	16" 41 cm	18" 46 cm	19" 48 cm	20" 51 cm	22" 56 cm	24" 61 cm	25" 64 cm	26" 66 cm
Yardage required (Color 1, Color 2)	345, 70	430, 80	530, 90	625, 100	740, 110	850, 120	1030, 130	1125, 140	1275, 150
Total yardage*	415	510	620	725	850	970	1160	1265	1425
Meters required (Color 1, Color 2)	315, 64	393, 74	485, 83	572, 92	677, 101	777, 110	942, 119	1029, 128	1166, 138
Total meters	379	467	568	664	778	887	1061	1157	1304

*The total yardage does not include the yarn for the flowers for the vest. Each flower uses about 2 yards (2 m) of yarn if you want to estimate how much yarn you'll need. For size 2, I made 27 flowers in a mix of five different colors.

This chart shows the finished garment measurements. The garment's waist circumference is its widest point, which encloses the lower back and waist. Because of this, you should choose a size with up to 6 inches (15 cm) of positive ease from your waist measurement. For reference, the model is 5 feet, 4 inches (163 cm) tall with a 36-inch (91-cm) chest and 27-inch (69-cm) waist and is wearing a size 2 with a finished garment waist measurement of 32 inches (81 cm) with 5 inches (13 cm) of positive ease. If between sizes, size down, or refer to Customized Sizing to get the perfect fit. Pattern sizes are written as 1 (2, 3, 4, 5) (6, 7, 8, 9). These sizes align with XS–5XL in the United States.

Customized Sizing

The Gardenia Vest consists of three panels: back, front right and front left. To change the waist circumference, you'll need to add or subtract starting chains from your back panel and front panels according to gauge. For example, if you want to add 2 inches (5 cm) to your waist circumference (8 dc), you'd need to add 1 inch (2.5 cm) to your back panel (4 dc) and 0.5 inch (1 cm) to each front panel (2 dc each).

To add length, simply add more rows to the body section in each panel according to gauge.

To increase the armhole gap size, add equal amounts of rows to increase the length in the back section for the back panel and front section for the front panels.

Back Panel

Body Section

Let's begin! With color 1, ch 55 (63, 70, 78, 86) (93, 101, 109, 116).

Row 1: Dc in 3rd ch from hook, work 1 dc in each ch to end of row. The 2 ch you skipped count as a dc, so you should now have 54 (62, 69, 77, 85) (92, 100, 108, 115) sts.

Row 2: Ch 2 (counts as your first dc here and throughout), turn, dc in each st down the row.

Repeat row 2 until you have 18 (18, 22, 22, 22) (24, 26, 26, 28) rows. Fasten off, but you're not done with this panel yet!

Back Section

For your next row, skip the first 10 (10, 14, 14, 14) (18, 18, 21, 21) sts, attaching your yarn on st 11 (11, 15, 15, 15) (19, 19, 22, 22). Ch 2, dc in next st and in each dc down the row until you have 10 (10, 14, 14, 14) (18, 18, 21, 21) sts left in the row. Leave remaining sts unworked, as seen in photo A. You'll now have 34 (42, 41, 49, 57) (56, 64, 66, 73) sts.

Repeat for row 2 across these middle stitches until you have 12 (14, 14, 16, 18) (20, 22, 24, 24) rows total in this back section, then fasten off (photo B).

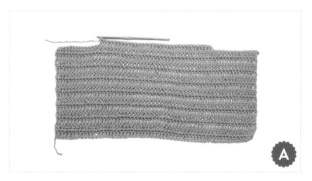

Front Right Panel

Body Section

Ch 28 (32, 36, 40, 44) (47, 51, 55, 59).

Row 1: Dc in the 3rd ch from the hook, then dc in each ch to end of row. The 2 ch you skipped counts as a dc, so you should now have 27 (31, 35, 39, 43) (46, 50, 54, 58) sts.

Row 2: Ch 2, turn, dc down the row. Each ch2 counts as your first dc. Repeat until you have 18 (18, 22, 22, 22) (24, 26, 26, 28) rows. Do not fasten off!

Front Section

For your next row, ch 2 and turn. Dc in each st down the row until you have 10 (10, 14, 14, 14) (18, 18, 21, 21) sts left in the row. Leave remaining sts unworked, with 17 (21, 21, 25, 29) (28, 32, 33, 37) sts worked.

Next 2 Rows: Ch 2 and turn, dc down the row (photo C).

Decrease Row: Ch 2 and turn. Dc in each st down the row until you have 4 sts left, dc2tog twice over last 4 sts. (2 sts decreased).

Non-Decrease Row: Ch 2 and turn. Dc in each st down the row.

Repeat previous 2 rows (alternating decrease and non-decrease) until you have 12 (14, 14, 16, 18) (20, 22, 24, 24) rows total in your front section, then fasten off (photo D). Final stitch count should be 9 (11, 11, 13, 15) (12, 14, 13, 17) sts.

Front Left Panel

Body Section

Ch 28 (32, 36, 40, 44, 47, 51, 55, 59).

Row 1: Dc in the 3rd ch from the hook, then dc in each ch to end of row. The 2 ch you skipped counts as a dc, so you should now have 27 (31, 35, 39, 43) (46, 50, 54, 58) sts.

Row 2: Ch 2, turn, dc down the row. Beginning ch 2 counts as your first dc. Repeat until you have 18 (18, 22, 22, 22) (24, 26, 26, 28) rows. Fasten off, but you're not done with this panel yet!

Front Section

Skip the next 10 (10, 14, 14, 14) (18, 18, 21, 21) sts, attaching your yarn on st 11 (11, 15, 15, 15) (19, 19, 22, 22). Ch 2, dc in the next st and each st down the row, as seen in photo E. In this section, you'll have 17 (21, 21, 25, 29) (28, 32, 33, 37) sts per row.

Next 2 Rows: Ch 2 and turn, dc down the row.

Decrease Row: Ch 2 (counts as first st) and turn. Dc2tog twice over next 4 sts. Dc in each st down the row.

Non-Increase Row: Ch 2, turn, dc down the row.

Repeat previous two rows until you have 12 (14, 14, 16, 18) (20, 22, 24, 24) rows total in this front section, then fasten off (photo F). Final stitch count should be 9 (11, 11, 13, 15) (12, 14, 13, 17) sts.

Congrats, you're done with all the body panels!

Assembly

I recommend using whip stitch (page 135) for all seaming, and to do all seaming with the wrong side facing you.

Lay your front panels on top of your back panels, lining up the last rows of your front panels with the last row of your back panel. Seam the shoulders by sewing the last row of your front panels to the last row of your back panel, starting from the outer edge and going in, then fasten off. Don't sew the sides together on this part!

Next, align the sides on the front panel's body sections with the sides on the back panel's body sections, as seen in photo G. Sew these sections together along the sides—don't sew the bottom (where the starting ch is) or top together!

Floral Decoration

Flower Stems

To create the flower stems, we're going to do some surface slip stitching, also known as surface crochet. If you've never done this before, don't worry! We're aiming for crooked stitches for a more organic look.

With color 2, create a slip knot and insert your hook into it. Identify where you want to place the bottom of your first flower stem; I recommend starting on the back.

Now, insert your hook into the foundation chain, going from the front of the panel down through to the back, as seen in photo H.

Pull the yarn from behind the panel through your panel and through the loop on your hook, creating your first surface slst (Photo I)!

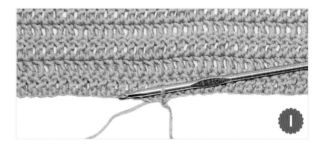

Continue to slst up the panel by first inserting the hook in the next place you want to slst, then pulling the yarn from behind the panel and through your hook to the surface, as seen in photos J and K. You can place them in a winding fashion, going left and right, becoming as long or as short as you'd like them to be. Once you're pleased with your stem's length, fasten off by cutting a 2-inch (5-cm) length of yarn and pulling it through the loop on your hook.

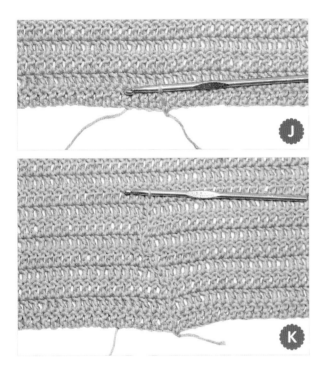

You can also make more stems branch off of your original one! To do this, create a slip knot and keep it behind your panel. Insert your hook into anywhere on an already-created stem instead of the foundation chain, then put the slip knot over your hook and pull to the surface. Then, continue to slip stitch as before to create a new stem. Continue this way until you're satisfied, then fasten off just like any normal stem.

Once you're satisfied with the number of stems you have, count the amount of stem endings (or how many times you fastened off). I made 27 on a size 2. We're going to make this many flowers! You need around 2 yds (2 m) for one flower.

Flowers

You can complete the flowers in any color you like! I used five different colors to make 27 different flowers.

To begin, ch 3.

Round 1: Working into 3rd ch from hook, (dc, ch 2, slst). This is your first petal (photo L). Continue working into same ch as last slst made. Work [ch 2, dc, ch 2, slst] until you have five petals total, as seen in photos M, N, O and P. Then, fasten off, leaving a 20-inch (51-cm) tail to sew the flower onto the vest (photo Q).

Tip: I recommend making your first ch as tight as possible; if it's too loose, the center of the flower may become too large.

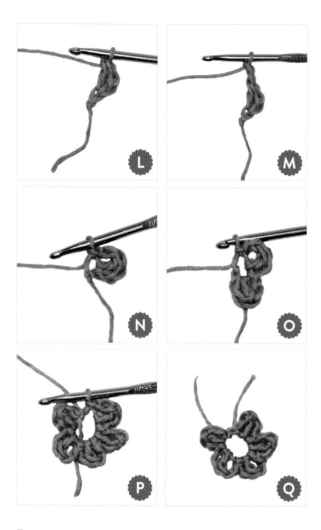

Final Details

To create the tie-front detail and to clean up the edges of your vest, place stitch markers where you want the tie-front detail to be. I placed mine on the third row of my front section of each front panel. Now, attach your yarn at any point on the bottom row of the back of your vest. Sc around the bottom until you come to the side of one of your front panels. To create a cleaner edge, place 3 sc in the bottom front corner of this panel. Sc up the side, placing approximately 2 sc in every 1 row of dc, until you come to your stitch marker.

Now, ch 60. You can chain more or less if you want a longer or shorter tie. Slst into each ch back to vest edge, then continue to sc around the front of the vest, around the top of the back, down to your next stitch marker, where you'll ch 60 again, slst in every ch, then continue to sc down the front of this panel. When you come to the other bottom front corner, place 3 sc in the corner. When you come to the place where you attached your yarn, slst into the top of your first sc and fasten off.

If you want this same clean edge on your arm holes, attach your yarn at any point and sc around, placing a slst into your first sc when you come back to it and fastening off. Repeat for the second arm hole.

Finally, weave in all your ends and—ta-da!—you're done!

Repeat to create the number of flowers you need to correspond to your stems. You're on the final stretch!

Once you've finished the flowers, you can begin sewing them on! To learn how to do so, see Sewing Appliques On (page 139). Repeat for your other flowers. This can be tedious, but the final look is worth it.

Spring Fling Shorts

Instantly wearable and easy to construct, the high-waisted Spring Fling Shorts are the perfect elevated staple. Out of all the patchwork designs in the book, this requires the least squares on average, so every time you make a square, you take one big step closer to having a comfortable and fashionable pair of shorts. The optional scalloped hems offer a fun finishing element to tie the whole look together or you can keep your hems straight and simple, depending on your personal style. Wear your shorts with a T-shirt for a simple summer look, or pair them with a turtleneck and boots for the days that dance between chilly and warm.

MATERIALS

Yarn
Worsted weight/size 4 yarn in 4 colors, 550–1185 total yds (504–1086 m). See specific yardage and meter amounts for each size in the pattern's size chart on page 41.

Shown In
Wool and the Gang Shiny Happy Cotton in the following colors:

* ✳ Color 1: Chalk Yellow
* ✳ Color 2: Ivory White
* ✳ Color 3: Lilac Wash
* ✳ Color 4: Eucalyptus Green

Hook
US H/8 (5 mm) or size needed to obtain gauge

Notions
Tapestry needle

Scissors

Stitch markers

Gauge
4 x 4" (10 x 10 cm) = 15 sts and 7.5 rows in double crochet

For swatch
Ch 21.

Row 1: Dc in 3rd st from hook (skipped sts count as dc) and in each st across, turn. [20 dc]

Row 2–10: Ch 2 (counts as first dc), dc in each st across, turn.

Block your swatch (page 146) if you plan on blocking your garment. Measure the inner 4 inches (10 cm) of your blocked swatch to get the most accurate measurement.

Spring Fling Shorts Sizing Chart

	Size 1	Size 2	Size 3	Size 4	Size 5	Size 6	Size 7	Size 8	Size 9
Finished waist measurement	25" 64 cm	30" 76 cm	35" 89 cm	40" 102 cm	45" 114 cm	50" 127 cm	55" 140 cm	60" 152 cm	65" 165 cm
Finished hip measurement	30" 76 cm	35" 89 cm	40" 102 cm	45" 114 cm	50" 127 cm	55" 140 cm	60" 152 cm	65" 165 cm	70" 178 cm
Finished thigh measurement	20" 51 cm	20" 51 cm	25" 64 cm	25" 64 cm	30" 76 cm	30" 76 cm	35" 89 cm	35" 89 cm	40" 102 cm
Yardage required (Color 1, Color 2, Color 3, Color 4)	50, 85, 135, 280	55, 95, 145, 300	65, 110, 175, 340	70, 120, 190, 355	80, 140, 215, 445	85, 150, 230, 465	105, 165, 260, 500	110, 175, 275, 520	120, 195, 300, 570
Total yardage required	550	595	690	735	880	930	1030	1080	1185
Meters required (Color 1, Color 2, Color 3, Color 4)	46, 78, 124, 256	51, 87, 133, 275	60, 101, 160, 311	64, 110, 174, 325	74, 128, 197, 407	78, 138, 211, 426	96, 151, 238, 458	101, 160, 252, 476	110, 179, 275, 522
Total meters required	504	546	632	673	806	853	943	989	1086
Number of squares	19	21	25	27	31	33	37	39	43

This chart shows the finished garment measurements. These shorts are meant to be slightly larger or fitted to your waist, hips and thighs. For reference, the model is 5 feet, 4 inches (163 cm) tall with a 27-inch (69-cm) waist, 36-inch (91-cm) hip and 22-inch (56-cm) thigh measurements, and is wearing a size 2 with customized sizing to add one square to each thigh (25" [64 cm] finished garment measurement) and to add 1 inch (2.5 cm) to the hips. Refer to Customized Sizing to do the same. If between sizes, size up. Pattern sizes are written as 1 (2, 3, 4, 5) (6, 7, 8, 9). These sizes align with XS–5XL in the United States.

Customized Sizing

The basic construction of the shorts is made of four components: the ring of squares that make up the waist, the ring of squares that make up the hips and the two rings of squares that make up the thighs. In the size chart, the hip ring is 1 square larger than the waist ring. If your measurements do not align with the standard sizing, you can make a custom-fit garment by following these steps.

First, take your waist, hip and thigh measurements and round up to the nearest multiple of 5 for inches, 13 for centimeters. For example, a 37-inch (94-cm) waist, 38-inch (97-cm) hip and 24-inch (61-cm) thigh would become a 40-inch (104-cm) waist, 40-inch hip (104-cm) and 25-inch (65-cm) thigh.

Next, divide each of these numbers by either 5 for inches or 13 for centimeters. These numbers would become 8 waist, 8 hip and 5 thigh for both measurements. Double the thigh number then add the waist and hip number and this is the number of squares you're going to make. In this example, you'd have 26 squares.

You'll follow the same construction pattern as the other sizes; just adjust according to your specific ring sizes. You can also adjust ring sizes by adding a couple inches. See Adding Length to Rows of Squares (page 136) for more details.

Base Square

The recommended square is the Starburst Granny Square (page 144), which is used in the sample. You can use any square you like that measures 5 x 5 inches (13 x 13 cm). Refer to the sizing section to see how many squares you're making in total, and complete that many. This is the longest step, but you can do it!

Beginning Assembly

The Spring Fling Shorts have a basic construction pattern: A ring of squares for the waist, a ring for the hips and a ring for each thigh. Use a whip stitch (page 135) for all seaming. I used color 4 for all seaming. Remember to always sew pieces together with the wrong sides facing out. Let's look at how we put it all together!

Thighs (make two)

Stitch together 4 (4, 5, 5, 6) (6, 7, 7, 8) squares to create a long row. Shown in photo A is a long row of 5 squares, perfect for sizes 3 and 4.

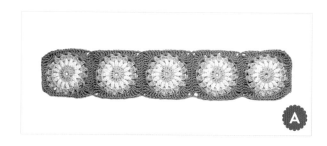

Waist

Stitch together 5 (6, 7, 8, 9) (10, 11, 12, 13) squares into a long row.

Hips

Stitch together 6 (7, 8, 9, 10) (11, 12, 13, 14) squares into a long row.

Body Assembly

Stitch your waist and hip rows together using the Whip Stitch Method (page 137).

Join together the now-attached waist and hip rows to form a ring, as seen in photo B. The seam you just created will be the front center of your shorts. This is your body ring.

Next, stitch together a thigh strip to form a ring. Repeat for the second thigh strip.

Now we will stitch the crotch area. Align the thigh rings and stitch them together on the top across one full square. One square should be long enough for most sizes. Only stitch the edge of the top of the squares together, as seen in photo C. If you want the crotch area to be shorter, only stitch together half a square. If you want it to be longer, stitch together half of another square.

Next, lay your body ring flat and put a stitch marker into the front center of your shorts at the bottom. Then, put another stitch marker parallel to this one on the opposite side of the body, as seen in photo D. There should be an equal amount of distance between the two stitch markers; for example, if the bottom of my body ring was 10 squares wide, there would be 5 squares in between each stitch marker.

Next, line up your attached legs under your body, putting the crotch where the stitch markers are. You will not sew the crotch into anything; instead, you will match the next unused stitch on the leg just in front or behind the crotch to the corresponding stitch marker. Stitch together the legs to the body one leg at a time, starting from one stitch marker until you reach the other, as seen in photos E and F. If the squares in the thigh ring and body ring do not match up exactly, you may need to apply the Whip Stitch Method (page 137).

Final Details

Creating the Waist Belt

After you've finished stitching both legs on, attach your yarn to the top of the waist.

Rounds 1–2: Ch 1 (does not count as a st), sc in each st around, slst to first st to join.

Round 3: Ch 3 (counts as a st), tc in each st around, slst to top of ch-3 to join.

Round 4: Ch 1, sc in each st around, slst to first st to join. Fasten off. (Photo G)

To create the waist chain that you'll use as a belt, first figure out how long you want it to be. I recommend adding 5–10 inches (12–25 cm) to your own waist measurement. Using color 4, ch 5 for every inch, or ch 2 for every cm; for example, for a 40-inch (102-cm) belt, ch 200. Slst into every chain, then fasten off. Weave in the ends.

To use the belt, start from the middle front of the shorts in the row of triple crochet. Weave the belt under a tc. Weave over the top of the next tc, then under the next. Repeat this all the way around until you finish, as seen in photo H, and tie in the front.

Optional Scallop Edges

Using color 4, make the scallop stitch (page 142) around the bottom of each leg and around the waist.

Note: If you have more than a difference of 1–2 inches (2–5 cm) between your waist measurement and the garment waist measurement, the scallop stitch may become distorted after tying the waist. To avoid this, skip 2 stitches instead of 1 during the scallop stitch when crocheting around the waist. You can follow as described for the thighs without distortion.

Weave in any loose ends you may still have, and congratulations! You're finished!

Ophelia Skirt

Ease your way into making crochet clothing with the Ophelia Skirt! Made with patchwork methods and colorful squares, this skirt is endlessly customizable and simple to construct. Its high waist and miniskirt length make it perfect for all occasions; you can dress it up or down to suit your needs. Make it in muted tones for a more sophisticated look, or create a fun color combination for an instant festival outfit. The patchwork look is tied together with the addition of scalloped hems and a simple cinched waist. Once the summer season ends, seamlessly incorporate it into your wardrobe by pairing it with a turtleneck and tights.

MATERIALS

Yarn

Worsted weight/size 4 yarn in 4 colors, 525–1565 total yds (481–1432 m). See specific yardage amounts for each size in the pattern's size chart on page 48.

Shown In

Modeled: Wool and the Gang Shiny Happy Cotton in the following colors:

* ✳ Color 1: Ivory White
* ✳ Color 2: Cameo Rose
* ✳ Color 3: Powder Blue
* ✳ Color 4: Eucalyptus Green

Step-by-Step: Red Heart Super Saver Yarn in the following colors:

* ✳ Color 1: Lemon
* ✳ Color 2: Soft White
* ✳ Color 3: Buff
* ✳ Color 4: Light Periwinkle

Hook

US H/8 (5 mm) or size needed to obtain gauge

Notions

Tapestry needle

Scissors

Stitch markers

Gauge

4 x 4" (10 x 10 cm) = 15 sts and 7.5 rows in double crochet

For swatch

Ch 21.

Row 1: Dc in 3rd st from hook (skipped sts count as dc) and in each st across, turn. [20 dc]

Row 2–10: Ch 2 (counts as first dc), dc in each st across, turn.

Block your swatch (page 146) if you plan on blocking your garment. Measure the inner 4 inches (10 cm) of your blocked swatch to get the most accurate measurement.

Ophelia Skirt Sizing Chart

	Size 1	Size 2	Size 3	Size 4	Size 5	Size 6	Size 7	Size 8	Size 9
Finished waist measurement	25" 64 cm	30" 76 cm	35" 89 cm	40" 102 cm	45" 114 cm	50" 127 cm	55" 140 cm	60" 152 cm	65" 165 cm
Finished hip measurement	30" 76 cm	35" 89 cm	40" 102 cm	45" 114 cm	50" 127 cm	55" 140 cm	60" 152 cm	65" 165 cm	70" 178 cm
Finished skirt length	17" 43 cm	17" 43 cm	17" 43 cm	17" 43 cm	17" 43 cm	22" 56 cm	22" 56 cm	22" 56 cm	22" 56 cm
Yardage required (Color 1, Color 2, Color 3, Color 4)	45, 80, 130, 270	55, 95, 140, 300	60, 110, 170, 330	70, 120, 190, 350	75, 135, 210, 400	115, 200, 315, 630	125, 220, 345, 680	135, 240, 375, 720	145, 260, 400, 760
Total yardage required	525	590	670	730	820	1260	1370	1470	1565
Meters required (Color 1, Color 2, Color 3, Color 4)	41, 74, 119, 247	51, 87, 128, 275	55, 101, 156, 302	64, 110, 174, 320	69, 124, 192, 366	106, 183, 288, 567	115, 202, 316, 622	124, 220, 343, 659	133, 238, 366, 695
Total meters required	481	541	614	668	751	1144	1255	1346	1432
Number of squares you'll make	18	21	24	27	30	45	49	53	57

This chart shows the finished garment measurements. This skirt is meant to be slightly larger or fitted to your waist and hip measurements. For reference, the model is 5 feet, 4 inches (163 cm) tall with a 27-inch (69-cm) waist and 36-inch (91-cm) hip measurements, and is wearing a size 2. If between sizes, size up, or refer to Customized Sizing to get the perfect fit. Pattern sizes are written as 1 (2, 3, 4, 5) (6, 7, 8, 9). These sizes align with XS–5XL in the United States.

Then, add on a third row that is 5 more than your hip for inches, 13 for centimeters. That would be 45 inches (117 cm). If you want your skirt to be 22 inches long (56 cm) instead of 17 inches (43 cm), you can add on a fourth row by doing the same thing again; in this example, the fourth row would then be 50 inches (130 cm).

Next, divide each of these numbers by either 5 for inches or 13 for centimeters. These numbers would become 8 waist, 8 hip, 9 third row and 10 fourth row for both measurements.

Finally, add up those numbers. In the example, we'd now have 25 for the shorter skirt and 35 for the longer skirt. This is the amount of squares you're going to make.

You'll follow the same construction pattern as the other sizes, just adjust according to your specific ring sizes.

Base Square

The recommended square is the Starburst Granny Square (page 144), which is used in the sample. You can use any square you like that measures 5 x 5 inches (13 x 13 cm). Refer to the sizing section to see how many squares you're making in total, and complete that many. This is the longest step, but you can do it!

Assembly

The Ophelia Skirt has a basic construction pattern: a ring of squares for the waist, a ring for the hips, a ring for the third row and a fourth row for sizes 6–9. Use a whip stitch (page 135) to seam your squares together. I used color 4 for all seaming. Remember to always sew pieces together with the wrong sides facing out. Let's look at how we put it all together!

Customized Sizing

The basic construction of the skirt is made of four components: the ring of squares that make up the waist, the ring of squares that make up the hips, which is generally one square larger than the waist, and the ring of squares that make up the third row. Sizes 6–9 also have a ring of squares that make up the fourth row. If your measurements do not align with the standard sizing, you can make a custom-fit garment by following these steps.

First, take your waist and hip measurements, and round up to the nearest multiple of 5 for inches, 13 for centimeters. For example, a 37-inch (94-cm) waist and 38-inch (97-cm) hip would become a 40-inch (104-cm) waist and 40-inch hip (104-cm).

Waist

Stitch together 5 (6, 7, 8, 9) (10, 11, 12, 13) squares to create a long row, as seen in photo A.

Hips

Stitch together 6 (7, 8, 9, 10) (11, 12, 13, 14) squares to create a long row.

Third Row

Stitch together 7 (8, 9, 10, 11) (12, 13, 14, 15) squares to create a long row.

Fourth Row (sizes 6, 7, 8 and 9 only)

Stitch together - (-, -, -, -) (12, 13, 14, 15) squares to create a long row.

Stitching it Together

Stitch your waist and hip rows together using the Whip Stitch Method (page 137).

Repeat this process to attach your third row to your combined waist-hip row. Make sure you attach it to the longer side of the combined waist-hip row. If you have a fourth row, add it on through the same process.

Join together the short ends of this panel to form a ring. The seam you just created will be the front center of your patchwork skirt.

Photo B shows the now-attached rows folded vertically before they are seamed together along that vertical line. Photo C shows the skirt once it's been seamed together to form the ring.

Final Details

Creating the Waist Belt

Attach your yarn anywhere on the top of the waist.

Rounds 1–2: Ch 1 (does not count as a st), sc in each st around, slst to first st to join.

Round 3: Ch 3 (counts as a st), tc in each st around, slst to top of ch-3 to join.

Round 4: Ch 1, sc in each st around, slst to first st to join. Fasten off (photo D).

For decoration, you can add either the scallop stitch (page 142) or extra rows of sc in color 4.

To create the waist belt, first figure out how long you want it to be. I recommend adding 5–10 inches (12–25 cm) to your own waist measurement.

Using color 4, ch 5 for every inch, or ch 2 for every cm; for example, for a 40-inch (102-cm) belt, ch 200. Slst into every chain, then fasten off. Weave in the ends.

To use the belt, start from the middle front of the skirt in the round of triple crochet. Weave the belt under a tc. Weave over the top of the next tc, then under the next, as seen in photo E. Repeat this all the way around until you finish, as seen in photo F, and tie in the front.

The Bottom Hem

For a clean finish, sc around the bottom of your skirt (the third or fourth row, depending on your size). For extra decoration, you can add either the scallop stitch (page 142) or extra rows of sc in colors of your choosing.

Weave in all ends and—ta-da!—you're done!

Dressed to the Nines

Unique styles deserve unique pieces, and you're sure to find a beauty or two to add to your wardrobe in this chapter. These elaborate-looking pieces are actually easy to construct, and everyone will be impressed that you made them yourself. For those with simple, laid-back styles, the Country-side Cardigan (page 79) is the way to go. Make it in monochrome, or dazzle with color blocking and stripes for some fun variations. To travel back in time, put on a pair of Solar Flares (page 55) or the Bell Blossom Top (page 63). Both of these patterns feature patchwork construction with floral squares and a knockout, '70s-inspired flare, sure to be admired by lovers of vintage styles. For a summer stunner, make the Gelato Sundress (page 87), which is simple in its stripes and tie-shoulder detail that is sure to flatter every body. The true standout, though, is the Daisy Daze Dress (page 71). The one-of-a-kind sleeves are fancy and floral, while the body is simple with a tie-waist silhouette and small floral details at the hem to tie in the gorgeous sleeves.

In this chapter, you will find a wide range of garments, all with one thing in common: They elevate your outfit. When you need a new statement piece to upgrade your wardrobe, don't buy it—make it!

Solar Flares

Just as eye-catching as a sunset, the Solar Flares elevate every outfit. The trendy flares and body-hugging silhouette combine to make a garment that suits a variety of situations, from daytime festivals to decades parties and nighttime outings. The patchwork construction creates a stunning starburst pattern, sure to garner compliments and catch eyes at any event. Go full-out '70s by pairing the piece with a flared sleeve top, or keep it simple with a crop top or T-shirt. No matter your body type, you can feel confident when you wear a pair of pants made just for you with the Solar Flares.

MATERIALS

Yarn
Worsted weight/size 4 yarn in 4 colors, 1165–1920 total yds (1066–1756 m). See specific yardage amounts for each size in the pattern's size chart on page 56.

Shown In
Hobbii Amigo XL in the following colors:

- ✳ Color 1: Sunflower
- ✳ Color 2: Ecru
- ✳ Color 3: Dusty Green
- ✳ Color 4: Wisteria

Hook
US H/8 (5 mm) or size needed to obtain gauge

Notions
Tapestry needle

Scissors

Stitch markers

Gauge
4 x 4" (10 x 10 cm) = 15 sts and 7.5 rows in double crochet

For swatch
Ch 21.

Row 1: Dc in 3rd st from hook (skipped sts count as dc) and in each st across, turn. [20 dc]

Row 2–10: Ch 2 (counts as first dc), dc in each st across, turn.

Block your swatch (page 146) if you plan on blocking your garment. Measure the inner 4 inches (10 cm) of your blocked swatch to get the most accurate measurement.

Solar Flares Sizing Chart

	Size 1	Size 2	Size 3	Size 4	Size 5	Size 6	Size 7	Size 8	Size 9
Finished waist measurement	25" 64 cm	30" 76 cm	35" 89 cm	40" 102 cm	45" 114 cm	50" 127 cm	55" 140 cm	60" 152 cm	65" 165 cm
Finished hip measurement	30" 76 cm	35" 89 cm	40" 102 cm	45" 114 cm	50" 127 cm	55" 140 cm	60" 152 cm	65" 165 cm	70" 178 cm
Finished thigh measurement	20" 51 cm	23" 58 cm	23" 58 cm	27" 69 cm	27" 69 cm	30" 76 cm	30" 76 cm	30" 76 cm	33" 84 cm
Finished mid-thigh measurement	17" 43 cm	17" 43 cm	21" 53 cm	23" 58 cm	23" 58 cm	27" 69 cm	27" 69 cm	27" 69 cm	30" 76 cm
Finished knee measurement	12" 30 cm	15" 38 cm	15" 38 cm	15" 38 cm	15" 38 cm	15" 38 cm	15" 38 cm	17" 43 cm	17" 43 cm
Finished inseam measurement	26" 66 cm	26" 66 cm	26" 66 cm	26" 66 cm	26" 66 cm	26" 66 cm	26" 66 cm	26" 66 cm	26" 66 cm
Yardage required (Color 1, Color 2, Color 3, Color 4)	115, 205, 315, 530	130, 230, 360, 585	140, 250, 385, 625	150, 265, 415, 660	155, 275, 430, 730	170, 305, 470, 790	175, 315, 485, 810	180, 325, 500, 825	190, 340, 525, 865
Total yardage required	1165	1305	1400	1490	1590	1735	1785	1830	1920
Meters required (Color 1, Color 2, Color 3, Color 4)	105, 188, 288, 485	119, 211, 330, 535	128, 229, 352, 572	137, 243, 380, 604	142, 252, 394, 668	156, 279, 430, 723	160, 288, 444, 741	165, 298, 458, 755	174, 311, 480, 791
Total meters required	1066	1195	1281	1364	1456	1588	1633	1676	1756
Number of squares	45	51	55	59	61	67	69	71	75

Abbreviations in US Crochet Terms

ch: chain

dc: double crochet

sc: single crochet

slst: slip stitch

st/sts: stitch/stitches

tc: triple crochet

This chart shows the finished garment measurements. The Solar Flares are meant to be slightly larger or fitted to your waist, hip and thigh measurements. The hem is meant to end at your ankle. For reference, the model is 5 feet, 4 inches (163 cm) tall with a 27-inch (69-cm) waist, 36-inch (91-cm) hip, 22-inch (56-cm) thigh, 16.5-inch (42-cm) mid-thigh, 14-inch (36-cm) knee and 25-inch (63.5-cm) inseam measurements, and is wearing a size 2. Refer to Customized Sizing to do the same. If between sizes, size up. Pattern sizes are written as 1 (2, 3, 4, 5) (6, 7, 8, 9). These sizes align with XS–5XL in the United States.

Measuring Tips for Solar Flares

When measuring the mid-thighs, hold the measuring tape 5–6 inches (13–15 cm) lower than where you measured the thighs, and go around the whole circumference of one thigh.

When measuring the knee, hold the measuring tape around the circumference of your knee.

When measuring the inseam, hold the measuring tape starting at your crotch/upper inner thigh and ending at the bottom of your ankle bone.

Customized Sizing

The basic construction of the Solar Flares is made of twelve components: the ring of squares that make up the waist, the ring that makes up the hips and is generally one square larger than the waist, the two rings that make up the thighs, the two rings that make up the mid-thighs, the two rings that make up the knees, the two rings that make up the first flare and the two rings that make up the final flare. If your measurements do not quite align with the standard sizing, you can make a custom-fit garment by following these steps.

First, take your waist, hip, thigh, mid-thigh and knee measurements, and divide them by 5 for inches, 13 for centimeters, and take note of the inches or centimeters left over.

For example:

* 37" (94 cm) waist = 7 squares + 2" (5 cm) waist
* 38" (97 cm) hip = 7 squares + 3" (8 cm) hip
* 24" (61 cm) thigh = 4 squares + 4" (10 cm) thigh
* 20" (51 cm) mid-thigh = 4 squares mid-thigh
* 17" (43 cm) knee = 3 squares + 2" (5 cm) knee

Next, add up the number of squares you'll need. Remember to double the numbers for the thigh, mid-thigh and knee to have enough squares for both legs. Do not add up the inches or centimeters left over. In our example, we'll have 36 squares so far. This number is how many squares you'll need to make the fitted part of the Solar Flares.

Next, we'll add on the number of squares for the flares. This is 4 per first flare, and 5 per final flare, so you'll add on 18 total. In our example, we would now have 54 squares.

If you want a longer inseam than 26 inches (66 cm), you'll need to either add rows of sc or dc at the end, or add another row of squares. Adding another row of squares will make the inseam 31" (79 cm) long. To do this, add a row that is 4 squares + 2.5 " (6 cm) long in between your first flare and final flare rows. In our example, we would now have 62 squares.

You now know how many squares you're going to make! You'll follow the same construction pattern as the other sizes, adjusted according to your specific ring sizes.

Base Square

The recommended square is the Starburst Granny Square (page 144), which is used in the sample. You can use any square you like that measures 5 x 5 inches (13 x 13 cm). Refer to the sizing section to see how many squares you're making in total, and complete that many. This is the longest step, but you can do it!

Row Assembly

Use a whip stitch (page 135) for all seaming. I used color 4 for all seaming. Remember to always sew pieces together with the wrong sides facing out. If you calculated Customized Sizing, add the inches or centimeters left over that you took note of to your rows of squares. To learn how to do this, see Adding Length to Rows of Squares on page 136. Let's look at how we put it all together!

Waist

Stitch together 5 (6, 7, 8, 9) (10, 11, 12, 13) squares into a long row. Pictured in photo A are 6 squares, perfect for size 2.

Hips

Stitch together 6 (7, 8, 9, 10) (11, 12, 13, 14) squares into a long row.

Thighs (make two)

Stitch together 4 (4, 4, 5, 5) (6, 6, 6, 6) squares to create a long row.

For sizes 2 and 3, add 3" (8 cm) to the end of your row.

For sizes 4 and 5, add 2" (5 cm) to the end of your row.

For size 9, add 3" (8 cm) to the end of your row.

For sizes 1, 6, 7 and 8, no length is added.

To learn how to add length to the end of a row of squares, see Adding Length to Rows of Squares on page 136.

Mid-Thighs (make two)

Stitch together 3 (3, 4, 4, 4) (5, 5, 5, 6) squares to create a long row.

For sizes 1, 2, 6, 7 and 8, add 2" (5 cm) to the end of your row.

For size 3, add 1" (2.5 cm) to the end of your row.

For sizes 4 and 5, add 3"(8 cm) to the end of your row.

For size 9, no length is added.

Knees (make two)

Stitch together 2 (3, 3, 3, 3) (3, 3, 3, 3) squares to create a long row.

For sizes 1, 8 and 9, add 2" (5 cm) to the end of your row. For sizes 2 through 7, no length is added.

First Flare Row (make two)

Stitch together 3 (4, 4, 4, 4) (4, 4, 4, 4) squares to create a long row.

For size 1 only, add 3" (8 cm) to the end of your row.

Second Flare Row (make two)

Stitch together 5 squares (all sizes).

Body Assembly

This is the home stretch! Stitch your waist and hip rows together using the Whip Stitch Method (page 137). Now, join the narrow ends of the waist-hip rows to form a ring, as seen in photo B. The seam you just created will be the front center of your Solar Flares. This is your body ring!

Now let's stitch together the rows to create the legs! Use the Whip Stitch Method (page 137) to do this. First, lay out your rows in order from top of the leg: Thigh, mid-thigh, knee, first flare, second flare. If you added length to multiple rows, place the sides with length on the same side (left or right side when laid out, as seen in photo C).

Stitch together the rows one at a time, working from the top of the leg (the thigh row) to the bottom (the second flare row), as seen in photo D. Repeat for the other leg.

Now, fold the leg in half along the length and sew closed using a whip stitch, as seen in photo E. Do not sew the bottom or top closed! Repeat for the other leg.

Now we will stitch the crotch area. Join the legs together by sewing together 5 inches (13 cm) on each leg from the thigh rows. If you added length to the thigh rows, include that part in the joined section. Only sew the edges of the tops of the thighs together, as seen in photo F. This forms the crotch.

Next, lay your body ring flat and put a stitch marker into the front center at the bottom (where it will join to the legs). Then, put another stitch marker parallel to this one on the opposite side of the body, as seen in photo G. There should be an equal amount of distance between the two stitch markers; for example, if the bottom of my body ring was 10 squares wide, there would be 5 squares in between each stitch marker.

Next, line up the attached legs under the body, putting the crotch where the stitch markers are. You will not sew the crotch into anything. Starting at one of the stitch markers, whip stitch the body ring to the leg until you reach the other stitch marker, skip over the crotch seam and continue to whip stitch the other side of the body to the other leg, as seen in photos H, I and J. You're almost done!

Final Details

Creating the Waist Belt

After you've finished stitching both legs on, attach your yarn to the top of the waist.

Rounds 1–2: Ch 1 (does not count as a st), sc in each st around, slst to first st to join.

Round 3: Ch 3 (counts as a st), tc in each st around, slst to top of ch-3 to join.

Round 4: Ch 1, sc in each st around, slst to first st to join. Fasten off. (Photo K)

To create the waist chain that you'll use as a belt, first figure out how long you want it to be. I recommend adding 5–10 inches (12–25 cm) to your own waist measurement.

Using color 4, ch 5 for every inch, or ch 2 for every cm; for example, for a 40-inch (102-cm) belt, ch 200. Slst into every ch, then fasten off. Weave in the ends.

To use the belt, start from the middle front of the Solar Flares in the row of triple crochet. Weave the belt over and under each tc all the way around the waist, as seen in photo L and tie in the front.

Optional Decoration

You have a couple of options for extra decoration after this. At the bottom of each leg and around the top of the pants, you can add a scallop stitch (page 142), extra rows of sc alternating in color, as pictured in photo M, or anything else you want! You can see the scallop stitch used around the waist in the modeled photos.

Note: If you have more than a difference of 1–2 inches (2–5 cm) between your waist measurement and the garment waist measurement, the scallop stitch may become distorted after tying the waist. To avoid this, skip 2 stitches instead of 1 during the scallop stitch when crocheting around the waist. You can follow as described for the bottom of the flares without distortion.

Weave in any loose ends you may still have, and congratulations! You're finished!

Bell Blossom Top

No retro collection is complete without a few flared sleeves! Reminiscent of the blooming, psychedelic imagery in music from the '60s and '70s, the Bell Blossom Top is perfect for adding flair to your wardrobe. Since it's a patchwork design, progress can be made any time you have a spare 20 minutes—the squares stack up quickly before they come together for an easy assembly. Make your own in bright colors to stand out on a dance floor or muted tones to go with any outfit you can dream up. With its boat neck, cinched waist and full sleeves, the Bell Blossom Top is flattering on everyone.

MATERIALS

Yarn

Worsted weight/size 4 yarn in 4 colors, 845–2195 total yds (774–2008 m). See specific yardage amounts for each size in the pattern's size chart on page 64.

Shown In

Modeled: Lion Brand Pima Cotton in the following colors:

* Color 1: Vintage
* Color 2: Pewter
* Color 3: Mademoiselle
* Color 4: Rose Taupe

Step-by-Step: Lion Brand Pima Cotton in the following colors:

* Color 1: Sand (discontinued)
* Color 2: Spice
* Color 3: Mineral Yellow
* Color 4: Blueprint

Hook

US H/8 (5 mm) or size needed to obtain gauge

Notions

Tapestry needle

2 stitch markers

Scissors

Gauge

4 x 4" (10 x 10 cm) = 15 sts and 7.5 rows in double crochet

For swatch

Ch 21.

Row 1: Dc in 3rd st from hook (skipped sts count as dc) and in each st across, turn. [20 dc]

Row 2–10: Ch 2 (counts as first dc), dc in each st across, turn.

Block your swatch (page 146) if you plan on blocking your garment. Measure the inner 4 inches (10 cm) of your blocked swatch to get the most accurate measurement.

Bell Blossom Top Sizing Chart

	Size 1	Size 2	Size 3	Size 4	Size 5	Size 6	Size 7	Size 8	Size 9
Finished chest circumference	30" 76 cm	35" 89 cm	40" 102 cm	45" 114 cm	50" 127 cm	55" 140 cm	60" 152 cm	65" 165 cm	70" 178 cm
Finished waist circumference	25" 64 cm	30" 76 cm	35" 89 cm	40" 102 cm	45" 114 cm	50" 127 cm	55" 140 cm	60" 152 cm	65" 165 cm
Total length measured from tops of shoulders	17" 43 cm	17" 43 cm	17" 43 cm	17" 43 cm	22" 56 cm	22" 56 cm	22" 56 cm	27" 69 cm	27" 69 cm
Upper arm circumference	10" 25 cm	13" 33 cm	13" 33 cm	15" 38 cm	15" 38 cm	15" 38 cm	20" 51 cm	20" 51 cm	20" 51 cm
Sleeve length measured from underarm	15" 38 cm	15" 38 cm	15" 38 cm	15" 38 cm	15" 38 cm	15"" 38 cm	15" 38 cm	15" 38 cm	15" 38 cm
Yardage required (Color 1, Color 2, Color 3, Color 4)	90, 160, 245, 350	100, 175, 270, 390	105, 185, 290, 410	125, 220, 345, 420	155, 275, 425, 580	165, 295, 455, 650	180, 320, 500, 715	220, 400, 620, 840	235, 420, 655, 885
Total yardage required	845	935	990	1110	1435	1565	1715	2080	2195
Meters required (Color 1, Color 2, Color 3, Color 4)	83, 147, 224, 320	92, 160, 247, 357	96, 170, 266, 375	115, 202, 316, 384	142, 252, 389, 531	151, 270, 416, 595	165, 293, 458, 654	202, 366, 567, 769	215, 384, 599, 810
Total meters required	774	856	907	1017	1314	1432	1570	1904	2008
Number of squares	35	39	41	49	61	65	71	88	93

Customized Sizing

The basic construction of the Bell Sleeve Top includes four panels: one front, one back and two sleeves. There are 9 different body sizes and 3 different sleeve sizes (one size for sizes 1–3, another for sizes 4–6, another for sizes 7–9).

The sleeve for sizes 1–3 uses 9 squares, the sleeve for sizes 4–6 uses 11 squares, and the sleeve for sizes 7–9 uses 12 squares. You can customize the number of squares to make a larger or smaller sleeve. For example, if you're making size 1–3 body but want a size 7–9 sleeve, add 6 squares (3 for each sleeve). If you're making size 7–9 body but want a size 1–3 sleeve, subtract 6 squares (3 for each sleeve). When you get to the Sleeves portion of the pattern, simply follow the instructions for one of the sizes in the sleeve range you chose.

Base Square

The Starburst Granny Square is recommended for this pattern. You can use any square you like, as long as it measures 5 x 5 inches (13 x 13 cm). Refer to the sizing section to see how many squares you're making in total, and complete that many. This is the longest step, but you can do it!

Panel Assembly

The Bell Blossom Top has a basic construction pattern: a back panel, a front panel and two sleeve panels. Use a whip stitch (page 135) for all seaming. I used color 4 for all seaming. Remember to always sew pieces together with the wrong sides facing out. Let's look at how we put it all together!

The chart on the previous page shows the finished garment measurements. The Bell Blossom Top is meant to be slightly larger or fitted to your chest, waist and upper arm measurements. For reference, the model is 5 feet, 4 inches (163 cm) tall with a 36-inch (91-cm) bust, 27-inch (69-cm) waist and 11-inch (28-cm) upper arm measurements, and is wearing a size 2. If between sizes, size up, or refer to Customized Sizing to get the perfect fit. Pattern sizes are written as 1 (2, 3, 4, 5) (6, 7, 8, 9). These sizes align with XS–5XL in the United States.

Front Panel

Both the front and back panels are made up of 3 rows (or 4 rows for sizes 5–9). Each row is stitched together one at a time to form the panel.

For row 1 (the top row, closest to shoulders), stitch together 3 (4, 4, 5, 5) (6, 6, 7, 7) squares to create a long row, as seen in photo A.

For row 2, stitch together 3 (4, 4, 5, 5) (6, 6, 7, 7) squares.

For row 3, stitch together 3 (3, 4, 4, 5) (6, 6, 7, 7) squares.

Sizes 5–9 only: For row 4, stitch together x (x, x, x, 4) (5, 5, 6, 7) squares.

Sizes 8–9 only: For row 5, stitch together x (x, x, x, x) (x, x, 6, 7) squares.

To create the panel, sew together two rows at a time. If your rows are different sizes, you'll need to use the Whip Stitch Method (page 137) to sew them together. Photo B shows a completed front panel for size 2.

Back Panel

For row 1 (the top row, closest to shoulders), stitch together 3 (4, 4, 5, 5) (6, 6, 7, 7) squares to create a long row.

For row 2, stitch together 3 (3, 4, 4, 5) (5, 6, 6, 7) squares.

For row 3, stitch together 2 (3, 3, 4, 5) (5, 6, 6, 7) squares.

Sizes 5–9 only: For row 4, stitch together x (x, x, x, 4) (5, 5, 6, 7) squares.

Sizes 8–9 only: For row 5, stitch together x (x, x, x, x) (x, x, 6, 7) squares.

Create the back panel as you did the front panel. Photo B shows a completed back panel for size 2.

Sleeves (make two)

Row 1: Stitch together 2 (2, 2, 3, 3) (3, 4, 4, 4) squares to create a row.

For sizes 2 and 3, add 3" (8 cm) to the end of row 1.

To learn how to add length to the end of a row of squares, see Adding Length to Rows of Squares on page 136.

Row 2: Stitch together 3 (3, 3, 4, 4) (4, 4, 4, 4) squares to create a row.

For sizes 7, 8 and 9, add 2" (5 cm) to the end of row 2.

Row 3: Stitch together 4 squares (all sizes).

For sizes 4, 5 and 6, add 3" (8 cm) to the end of row 3.

For sizes 7, 8 and 9, add 4" (10 cm) to the end of row 3.

Use the Whip Stitch Method (page 137) to sew the rows together into panels (photo D).

Tip: For sizes 1–4, if you want even more of a flare and longer sleeves, you can create a fourth row of 5 squares to add on.

Final Assembly

Shoulder Shaping

Place a stitch marker in the exact middle of the top of your back panel. Measure 5 inches (13 cm) from the center out on both sides and place a stitch marker at each point so they're 10 inches (26 cm) apart, as seen in photo E.

Attach your yarn to the top left or right corner of your back panel.

Row 1: Ch 2, dc in each st toward the middle until you hit the stitch marker.

Rows 2–4: Ch 2, turn, dc in each st across.

Fasten off, and leave a length of yarn long enough to sew across the entire row (about 1 yd; photo F).

Repeat on the other side of the top row of your back panel, then whip stitch the added dc sections to the corresponding sides on the top row of the front panel, as seen in photo G.

Body Assembly

Next, we'll sew the sleeves onto the body. On the outer edge of your added 4 dc rows, add a stitch marker in the middle of the 4 rows so 2 rows will be on either side of the marker. On your sleeve, put a stitch marker in the middle of your top row (upper arm). Line up the stitch markers as seen in photo H, then sew the sleeve onto the body so that the stitch markers are still aligned (photo I).

Repeat this process for the other side with the other sleeve.

Next, we'll do our final sewing bit (yay!). Fold your piece in half and, starting from the outer edge of one sleeve, sew the sleeve closed working toward the armpit, then toward the bottom of the body, as seen in photo J. Repeat for the other sleeve.

Final Details

Finishing the Neck

It's quite simple: Attach your yarn at any point on your neckline, ch 1, sc in the same stitch, then sc around the neckline. At the added dc sections, work 2 sc for every 1 dc row. Slst into your first sc once you've completed the neck and fasten off for a clean finish.

Waist Band

Attach your yarn at any point on the bottom of the body.

Rounds 1–3: Ch 1, sc in the same stitch, sc in each st around, slst to first st to join. I used color 4 for rows 1 and 3, and color 2 for row 2.

Round 4: Ch 3 (counts as first tc), tc in each sc around, slst to first tc to join. I used color 4.

Rounds 5–7: Repeat rounds 1–3. Fasten off. I used color 4 for rows 5 and 7, and color 2 for row 6 (photo K).

Waist Belt

To create the waist chain that you'll use as a belt, first figure out how long you want it to be. I recommend adding 5–10 inches (12–25 cm) to your own waist measurement.

Using color 4, ch 5 for every inch, or ch 2 for every cm; for example, for a 40-inch (102-cm) belt, ch 200. Slst into every ch, then fasten off. Weave in the ends.

To use the belt, start from the middle back of your top in the row of tc. Weave the belt over and under each tc all the way around the waist, as seen in photos L and M, then tie in the back.

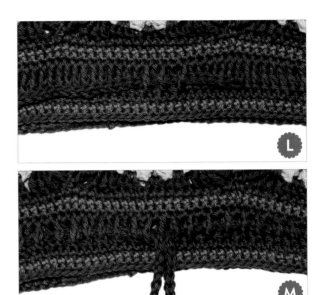

Sleeve Cuffs

To get a cleaner finish on your sleeves, you can add 5 sc rounds around each cuff. Work similar to round 1 of Waist Band for 5 total rounds, as seen in photo N.

Weave in any loose ends you may have, and congrats! You're finished!

Daisy Daze Dress

The perfect piece to dress up for a semiformal event or dress down for a casual picnic, the Daisy Daze Dress is a versatile addition to your wardrobe. The simple body construction allows for mindless, meditative crocheting before you move on to the centerpiece of the dress: the sleeves! To complete your outfit on a chilly day, layer it with a plain long-sleeve shirt underneath and leggings. For warm afternoons, all you need is a simple slip underneath. With a flattering tie-waist and small floral details along the bottom hem to balance out the eye-catching sleeves, this dress is sure to get you compliments wherever it goes.

MATERIALS

Yarn
Worsted weight/size 4 yarn in 3–4 colors, 1142–2695 total yds (1044–2465 m). See specific yardage amounts for each size in the pattern's size chart on page 72.

Shown In
Lion Brand 24/7 Cotton in the following colors:

* ✳ Color 1 (Dress Base): Navy
* ✳ Color 2 (Flower Center): Ecru
* ✳ Color 3 (Flower Petals): Sky and Bayleaf

Hook
US H/8 (5 mm) or size needed to obtain gauge

Notions
Tapestry needle

Stitch markers

Scissors

Gauge
4 x 4" (10 x 10 cm) = 14.5 sts and 8 rows in double crochet

For swatch
Ch 21.

Row 1: Dc in 3rd st from hook (skipped sts count as dc) and in each st across, turn. [20 dc]

Row 2–10: Ch 2 (counts as first dc), dc in each st across, turn.

Block your swatch (page 146) if you plan on blocking your garment. Measure the inner 4 inches (10 cm) of your blocked swatch to get the most accurate measurement.

Daisy Daze Dress Sizing Chart

	Size 1	Size 2	Size 3	Size 4	Size 5	Size 6	Size 7	Size 8	Size 9
Finished body circumference	32" 81 cm	36" 91 cm	40" 102 cm	44" 112 cm	48" 122 cm	52" 132 cm	56" 142 cm	60" 152 cm	65" 165 cm
Total length measured from tops of shoulders	28" 71 cm	28" 71 cm	30" 76 cm	30" 76 cm	32" 81 cm	32" 81 cm	34" 86 cm	34" 86 cm	36" 91 cm
Sleeve length	21" 53 cm	21" 53 cm	21" 53 cm	21" 53 cm	21" 53 cm	16" 41 cm	16" 41 cm	16" 41 cm	16" 41 cm
Sleeve width	12" 30 cm	12" 30 cm	12" 30 cm	18" 46 cm	18" 46 cm	18" 46 cm	24" 61 cm	24" 61 cm	24" 61 cm
Yardage required (Color 1, Color 2, Color 3)	945, 76, 120	1055, 78, 123	1270, 80, 127	1400, 102, 161	1615, 104, 164	1745, 86, 135	2015, 103, 162	2150, 105, 165	2420, 107, 168
Total yardage required	1142	1256	1477	1663	1883	1966	2280	2420	2695
Meters required (Color 1, Color 2, Color 3)	864, 70, 110	965, 71, 151	1161, 73, 116	1280, 93, 147	1477, 95, 150	1596, 79, 124	1843, 94, 148	1966, 96, 151	2213, 98, 154
Total meters required	1044	1187	1350	1520	1723	1799	2085	2213	2465

This chart shows the finished garment measurements. This dress is made of rectangle panels sewn together to make the body. This means that the dress measures the same at every point—chest, waist, hips, etc. To get the perfect fit, you'll want to choose the size that is closest to or slightly larger than the widest measurement on your body. For reference, the model is 5 feet, 11 inches (180 cm) tall with a 36-inch (91-cm) chest, 30-inch (76-cm) waist, 40-inch (102-cm) hip and 11-inch (28-cm) upper arm measurements, and is wearing a size 3. If between sizes, size up, or refer to Customized Sizing to get the perfect fit. Pattern sizes are written as 1 (2, 3, 4, 5) (6, 7, 8, 9). These sizes align with XS–5XL in the United States.

Abbreviations in US Crochet Terms

ch: chain
dc: double crochet
sc: single crochet
slst: slip stitch
st/sts: stitch/stitches

Customized Sizing

The Daisy Daze Dress consists of four panels: one for the front, one for the back and one for each sleeve. If you'd like to make your dress slightly wider/narrower, simply add or subtract dc to your initial starting chain according to gauge. For example, if you want to add 2 inches (5 cm) in width (7 dc) to your widest point measurement, you'd need to add 1 inch (2.5 cm) in width to both body panels, which would be adding 4 dc to one panel and 3 dc to the other. Same applies to length. If you want to change your sleeve width, you can follow the instructions for the size larger/smaller than you.

Body Panels (make two)

With color 1, ch 59 (66, 74, 81, 88) (95, 103, 110, 119).

Row 1: Dc in the third ch from the hook (skipped chs count as a dc), dc in each ch to end. You should now have 58 (65, 73, 80, 87) (94, 102, 109, 118) sts.

Row 2: Ch 2 (counts as a dc), turn, dc in each st across.

Repeat row 2 until you have 56 (56, 60, 60, 64) (64, 68, 68, 72) rows. Fasten off, and you've finished one panel! Repeat for the back.

Sleeve Flowers

With color 2, ch 4, slst into first ch to form a ring.

Round 1: Ch 2 (counts as first dc), dc 15 into ring, with color 3 slst into first dc (the initial ch 2). [16 dc]

Note: You can fasten off color 2 after you slst with color 3. See page 139 for tips on color changes.

Round 2: [Ch 16, slst into same st, slst into next st] around until you have 16 petals total, then ch 1 and fasten off.

Create a total of 24 (24, 24, 32, 32) (24, 30, 30, 30) flowers. If you have two different colors for the Flower Petal yarn, create half in one color and half in the other.

Hem Flowers

With color 2, ch 4, slst into first ch to form a ring.

Round 1: Sc 8 into ring, with color 3 slst into first sc. [8 sc]

Round 2: [Ch 8, slst into same st, slst into next st] around until you have 8 petals total, then ch 1 and fasten off.

Create a total of 8 (9, 10, 11, 12) (13, 14, 15, 16) flowers. If you have two different colors for color 3 like I did, create half in one color and half in the other.

Assembly

I recommend the Whip Stitch Method (page 137) for all seaming. Make sure you always seam with the wrong sides facing out.

Neck Shaping/Attaching the Panels

Place a stitch marker in the exact middle of the top of one of your body panels. Measure 5 inches (13 cm) out from either side of the marker and place two stitch markers in those spots so they're 10 inches (26 cm) apart.

With color 1, attach your yarn to the top left or right corner of your back panel.

Row 1: Ch 2 (counts as a dc), then dc in each st toward the middle until you hit the stitch marker.

Rows 2–5: Ch 2 (counts as a dc), turn, dc in each st across row.

Fasten off, and leave a length of yarn long enough to sew across the entire row (30 in [76 cm]), as seen in photo A.

Repeat on the other corner of this panel, then seam the added dc sections to the corresponding sides on the top row of your other body panel.

Creating the Sleeves

Line two flowers up and cut two small (6-inch [15-cm]) pieces of yarn of color 3. Tie two of the petals together at their apex, as seen in photo B.

Including these two flowers, arrange four flowers into a square. Connect each of the flowers together as seen in photo C. The diagonal connections are done via slst, and the vertical/horizontal connections are done via tying the petals together.

To slst two petals together, first slst into the apex of one of the petals. Ch 8 as seen in photo D, then slst into the petal you want to connect it to. Cut your yarn and pull through the loop to fasten off, as seen in photo E.

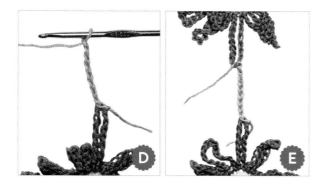

Continue to attach flowers and arrange in the following order:

* Sizes 1–3: 3 flowers tall x 4 flowers wide
* Sizes 4–5: 4 flowers tall x 4 flowers wide
* Size 6: 4 flowers tall x 3 flowers wide
* Sizes 7–9: 5 flowers tall x 3 flowers wide

In photo F, you can see an arrangement of a panel that is 3 flowers tall and 4 flowers wide, perfect for sizes 1–3.

Repeat for the second sleeve.

Preparing the Sleeves

Now we'll prepare the sleeves to be attached to the body. To do this, on your edge flowers (the ones with petals still loose because they're on the edge), tie together an extra petal from each flower so there are three petals sewn together for each edge flower, as seen in photo G. This should leave eight petals loose on your corner flowers and four petals loose on your edge flowers.

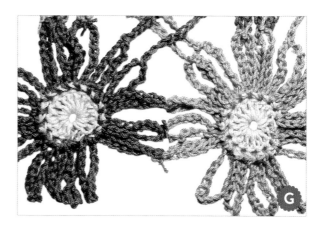

Identify one of your corner flowers on the tall edge (the edge with three flowers for sizes 1–3, 4 for 4–6 and 5 for 7–9). Section your flower into 4 petals pointing toward the wide edge and 4 pointing toward the tall edge. Slst with color 1 onto the outermost petal on the tall edge (photo H).

Connecting Row: *[Ch 3, slst into the next petal] three times to connect petals of one flower, then ch 8 and slst into the petal on the next flower; repeat from * until worked across all petals for this side. (Photos I, J)

Note: For the last flower in your row, the other corner flower, only attach four of the petals (like you did for the first corner flower), ch 1, fasten off.

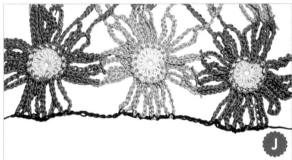

Repeat for the second sleeve.

Attaching the Sleeves

Next, we'll sew the sleeves onto the body. On the outer edge of your added 5 dc rows, add a stitch marker in the third row.

Line up your sleeve so the middle of the long edge where you joined the flowers is aligned with the stitch marker, as seen in photo L. Starting from the stitch marker and going out toward the edges, sew the slst row onto the body, as seen in photo M. Repeat for the other sleeve.

Closing the Sleeves

Step 1: Fold the body in half, including the sleeves. Align the sleeves so the petals all align on the bottom edge. Just as you did before, section off the corner flowers into four petals pointing lengthwise and four pointing widthwise (technically, there will be eight petals total, since you've folded the sleeve in half so flowers are sitting on top of one another), as seen in photo N.

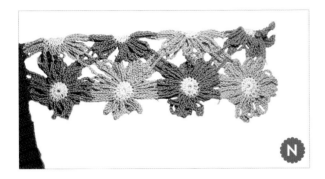

Step 2: Align the petals that are lying on top of one another and pointing lengthwise. You'll now be slip stitching these flowers' petals together to close the sleeve.

Note: In the next step, make sure you're actually slip stitching two petals together when you slst into a new petal.

Step 3: With color 3, working around both layers of petals, slst onto the outermost petals on the length edge (near the wrist), as seen in photo O. * [Ch 3, slst into both layers of the next petal] three times, ch 8 and slst into both of the first petals on the next flower. Repeat from * up sleeve from wrist to armpit, as seen in photo P. (ch 3 in between petals, ch 8 in between flowers)

Step 4: When you've done your last slst into a petal, ch 8 and slst onto both panels of the body at the same place, approximately 2 inches (5 cm) down from the petal pointing widthwise, as seen in photo Q. Repeat for the other sleeve.

To create a cleaner cuff edge, slst into the first petal that you did in step 3 again, but go into only one flower, not both. *[Ch 3, then slst into the next petal of the same flower on the width edge (the petals that are still loose)] until the end of that flower's petals, then ch 8 and slst into the next flower's first petal. Repeat from * around, then slst back into the first slst made for this cuff. If desired, sc in each ch around for a thicker cuff edge, then slst into first sc and fasten off (photo R).

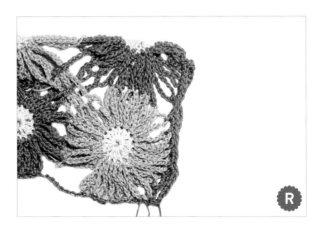

Final Details

Sewing the Sides

Using color 1 and working from the bottom hem up, whip stitch the sides of your dress together, stopping where you had slipstitched the sleeve onto the body.

Hem Flowers

Before sewing your flowers onto the hem, space them evenly to get a visual of how you'd like to place them. I placed mine so that the top of the flower is 1.5 inches (4 cm) above the bottom hem, and the flowers are 1.5 inches (4 cm) apart as seen in photo S. Sew them on with the same color yarn of the petals. See Sewing Appliques On (page 139) for more tips.

Waist Belt

Try on your dress and place a stitch marker in the row where you want your waist belt to be.

To create the waist chain that you'll use as a belt, first figure out how long you want it to be. I recommend adding 5–10 inches (12–25 cm) to your own waist measurement. Using color 1, ch 5 for every inch, or ch 2 for every cm; for example, for a 40-inch (102-cm) belt, ch 200. Slst into every chain, then fasten off. Weave in the ends.

To use the belt, start from the middle back of your dress in the row of dc that you had marked. Weave the belt under a dc, then over the top of the next dc, then under the next. Repeat this all the way around until you finish, as seen in photo T, then tie in the back.

Finishing the Neck

Attach your yarn at any point on your neckline, ch 1, sc in the same stitch, then sc around the neckline. At the added dc sections, work 2 sc for every 1 dc row. Slst into your first sc once you've completed the neck and fasten off for a clean finish.

Weave in any loose ends you may have, and congrats! You're finished!

Countryside Cardigan

Named for the simplicity found in the countryside, the Countryside Cardigan is a versatile layering piece you can wear all year. This unisex design features a button-up front and an understated collar that brings a boost to any outfit. For a timeless look, you can make it in a solid color; for a modern take, color block different sections to create a cardigan like no other. Endlessly customizable and sure to become a repeat wear, the Countryside Cardigan is a necessary staple for your handmade collection.

MATERIALS

Yarn
Worsted weight/size 4 yarn in 1 color, 780–2315 total yds (713–2117 m). See specific yardage amounts for each size in the pattern's size chart on page 81.

Shown In
Wool and the Gang Shiny Happy Cotton in Eucalyptus Green

Hook
US H/8 (5 mm) or size needed to obtain gauge

Notions
6–8 buttons (0.5" [1 cm] each)

Tapestry needle

Scissors

Stitch markers

Gauge
4 x 4" (10 x 10 cm) = 15.5 sts and 8 rows in double crochet

4 x 4" (10 x 10 cm) = 14 sts and 20 rows in single crochet

For double crochet swatch:
Ch 21.

Row 1: Dc in 3rd st from hook (skipped sts count as dc) and in each st across, turn. [20 dc]

Rows 2–10: Ch 2 (counts as first dc), dc in each st across, turn.

For single crochet swatch:
Ch 21.

Row 1: Sc in 2nd st from hook and in each st across, turn. [20 sc]

Rows 2–22: Ch 1, sc in each st across, turn.

Block your swatches (page 146) if you plan on blocking your garment. Measure the inner 4 inches (10 cm) of your blocked swatches to get the most accurate measurement.

Countryside Cardigan Sizing Chart

	Size 1	Size 2	Size 3	Size 4	Size 5	Size 6	Size 7	Size 8	Size 9
Finished chest circumference	34" 86 cm	38" 97 cm	42" 107 cm	46" 117 cm	50" 127 cm	54" 137 cm	58" 147 cm	62" 157 cm	66" 168 cm
Upper arm circumference	14" 36 cm	14" 36 cm	16" 41 cm	18" 46 cm	18" 46 cm	20" 51 cm	20" 51 cm	22" 56 cm	22" 56 cm
Sleeve length measured from underarm	6" 15 cm	6" 15 cm	6" 15 cm	6" 15 cm	4" 10 cm	4" 10 cm	4" 10 cm	4" 10 cm	4" 10 cm
Total lengths measured from tops of shoulders	18" 46 cm	20" 51 cm	20" 51 cm	22" 56 cm	24" 61 cm	24" 61 cm	26" 66 cm	28" 71 cm	30" 76 cm
Yardage required	780	945	1095	1285	1400	1535	1770	2040	2315
Meters required	713	864	1001	1175	1280	1404	1619	1865	2117

Sizing Chart

This chart shows the finished garment measurements. This top is designed to be worn with up to 6 inches (15 cm) of positive ease, depending on the size you are making. Find the finished chest measurement in this chart and refer to the built-in ease when choosing a size to make. For reference, the model is 5 feet, 4 inches (163 cm) tall with a 34.5-inch (88-cm) chest and 10-inch (25-cm) upper arm measurements and is wearing a size 2 (resulting in 3.5 inches [9 cm] of positive ease). If between sizes, size up, or refer to Customized Sizing to get the perfect fit. Pattern sizes are written as 1 (2, 3, 4, 5) (6, 7, 8, 9). These sizes align with XS–5XL in the United States.

Abbreviations in US Crochet Terms

ch = chain
dc = double crochet
sc = single crochet
sk = skip
slst = slip stitch
st/sts = stitch/stitches

Customized Sizing

The Countryside Cardigan consists of five panels: back panel, two front panels worked directly onto the back panel and two sleeve panels. If you'd like to change the chest circumference, add stitches to your foundation chain according to gauge. For example, if you want to add 2 inches (5 cm) in width (16 dc), you'd need to add 1 inch (2.5 cm) in width to the back panel. Since the front panels are worked directly onto the back, you'll add an extra 8 dc per panel. The same applies to changing the upper arm circumference.

To add or subtract length to your cardigan, add or subtract an equal number of rows to both the back panel and the front panels according to gauge. For example, to add 1 inch (2.5 cm) in length, add two rows to each panel.

If you want to follow a different body size than a sleeve size, simply follow the size you want to for both the front and back panel sections for the body, then follow the size you want to for the sleeves section.

Back Panel

Let's begin! Ch 65 (73, 81, 88, 96) (104, 112, 119, 127).

Row 1: Dc in third ch from hook (skipped chs count as dc here and throughout), dc in each ch to end. You should now have 64 (72, 80, 87, 95) (103, 111, 118, 126) sts.

Row 2: Ch 2 (counts as your first dc), turn, dc to end.

Repeat row 2 until you have 36 (40, 40, 44, 48) (48, 52, 56, 60) rows. After your last back row, do not fasten off, continue on to front panels.

Front Panels

Row 1: Ch 2 (counts as a dc), dc in next 15 (19, 25, 27, 30) (34, 38, 42, 46) sts.

Row 2: Ch 2 and turn. Dc to end.

Row 3: Ch 2 and turn. Dc to last 2 sts, 2 dc in each of last two sts. You should now have 18 (22, 28, 30, 33) (37, 41, 45, 49) sts.

Row 4: Ch 2 and turn. Dc to end.

Row 5: Ch 2 and turn. Dc to last 2 sts, 2 dc in each of last two sts. You should now have 20 (24, 30, 32, 35) (39, 43, 47, 51) sts (photo A).

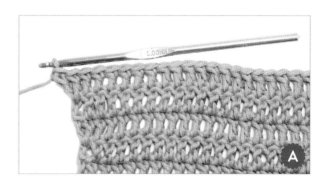

Row 6: Ch 2 and turn. Dc to end.

Row 7: Ch 2 and turn. Dc to last 2 sts, 2 dc in each of last two sts. You should now have 22 (26, 32, 34, 37) (41, 45, 49, 53) sts.

Row 8: Ch 2 and turn. Dc to end.

Row 9: Ch 2 and turn. Dc to last 2 sts, 2 dc in each of last two sts. You should now have 24 (28, 34, 36, 39) (43, 47, 51, 55) sts. Place a stitch marker in the last stitch in this row for future reference.

Row 10: Ch 2 and turn, dc to end.

Repeat row 10 until you have a total of 36 (40, 40, 44, 48) (48, 52, 56, 60) rows in this front panel section. After your last row, fasten off.

Attach your yarn to the other side of your back panel and repeat to create second front panel. Fasten off.

Sleeves (make two)
Ch 53 (53, 62, 69, 69) (77, 77, 85, 85).

Row 1: Dc in third ch from hook (skipped chs count as dc here and throughout), dc in each ch to end. You should now have 52 (52, 61, 68, 68) (76, 76, 84, 84) sts.

Row 2: Ch 2 (counts as first dc), turn, dc to end.

Repeat row 2 until you have 12 (12, 12, 12, 8) (8, 8, 8, 8) rows.

Fasten off. Repeat for the second sleeve.

Attaching the Sleeves

Remember to do all seaming with the wrong side facing out. I recommend the Whip Stitch Method (page 137) for seaming.

Place a stitch marker in the exact middle of the top of one of your sleeve panels. On the outer edge of your top, place a stitch marker in between the rows that ended the back panel and began the front panel. Line up the stitch markers as seen in photo B, then sew the sleeve onto the body so that the stitch markers are still aligned (photo C). Two sleeve stitches will go into one row of dc on the body. Repeat on the other side.

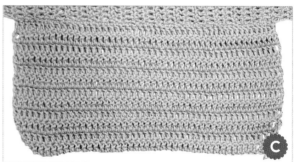

Fold the cardigan in half so that the body panels are on top of each other and the sleeve panels are folded in half (photo D). Starting on the outer corner of the sleeve, seam the sleeve closed going toward the body, then down the body going toward the hem. Repeat on the other side.

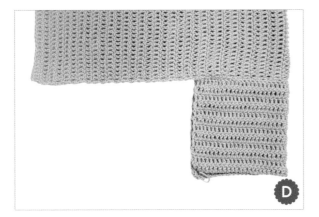

Final Details

Button Band

Attach your yarn to the bottom front corner of one of the panels.

Row 1: Ch 1 (does not count as a st here and throughout), sc evenly along the side (about 2 sc for every 1 row of dc) until you reach the stitch marker you placed earlier (photos E and F). After you reach the stitch marker, remove it.

Rows 2–4: Ch 1 and turn. Sc in each st across. Fasten off (photo G).

Button-Hole Band

Attach your yarn to the bottom front corner of the other panel.

Row 1: Ch 1 (does not count as a st), sc evenly along the side (about 2 sc for every 1 row of dc) until you reach the stitch marker you placed earlier. After you reach the stitch marker, remove it.

Row 2: Ch 1 and turn. Sc 4, ch 2 (photo H), sk 2 sts. *sc 6, ch 2, sk 2 sts*. Repeat from * to * down the row (photos I and J). The gaps you're making when you ch 2 then skip 2 sts before you sc again are your button holes.

Row 3: Ch 1 and turn. Sc in each sc and work 2 sc in each ch-2 sp across.

Row 4: Ch 1 and turn. Sc in each st across. Fasten off (photo K).

Sew your buttons onto the button band, aligning them with the gaps on the other band.

Collar

Attach your yarn to the top outer edge of one of your button bands.

Row 1: Ch 1, sc all the way around the neck opening until you reach the outer edge of the other button band, as seen in photo L.

Row 2: Ch 1, turn, sc to end.

Repeat row 2 for as many rows as you like to create the collar. I did 10 rows. Fold it over to achieve the perfect folded collar look, as seen in photo M.

Cleaning Up the Edges

Attach your yarn to the bottom of the cardigan at the bottom outer edge of one of your button bands. Sc evenly around the bottom, then fasten off.

Attach your yarn to the bottom of a sleeve. Sc evenly all the way around, then slst into the first sc and fasten off. Repeat on the other sleeve.

Weave in all loose ends, and congratulations! You're done!

Gelato Sundress

Simple to make and elegant to wear, the Gelato Sundress is made for crocheters looking for a mindless project that ends in a beautiful fashion statement. The tie-shoulder straps make this design easy to slip on and adjust to your preference, while the ties at both the waist and top help to create a classic and comfortable silhouette. You can switch up the pattern by making it two-tone, or go all out and make each section wholly unique! With straightforward stripes and clean, straight hems, the Gelato Sundress is a classic design that will stand the test of time.

MATERIALS

Yarn

Worsted weight/size 4 yarn in 2–8 colors, 1525–4655 total yds (1395–4257 m). See specific yardage amounts for each size in the pattern's size chart on page 89.

Shown In

Wool and the Gang Shiny Happy Cotton in the following colors:

* ✳ Base Color: Ivory White
* ✳ Stripes: Mellow Mauve, Duck Egg Blue, Purple Haze, Lilac Wash, Powder Blue

Hook

US H/8 (5 mm) or size needed to obtain gauge

Notions

Tapestry needle

Stitch markers

Scissors

Gauge

4.5 x 4.5" (11.5 x 11.5 cm) = 15 sts and 7.5 rows in double crochet

4.5 x 4.5" (11.5 x 11.5 cm) = 14 sts and 15 rows in griddle stitch

For double crochet swatch

Ch 21.

Row 1: Dc in 3rd st from hook (skipped sts count as dc) and in each st across, turn. [20 dc]

Rows 2–10: Ch 2 (counts as first dc), dc in each st across, turn.

For griddle stitch swatch

Ch 21.

Row 1: Sc in 2nd st from hook, dc in next st. Alternate [sc, dc] in each st across, turn. [20 sts]

Rows 2–20: Ch 1 (does not count as sc), [sc, dc] in each st across, turn.

For more explanation on the griddle stitch, see page 140.

Block your swatches (page 146) if you plan on blocking your garment. Measure the inner 4 inches (10 cm) of your blocked swatches to get the most accurate measurement.

Gelato Sundress Sizing Chart

	Size 1	Size 2	Size 3	Size 4	Size 5	Size 6	Size 7	Size 8	Size 9
Finished body circumference	34" 86 cm	36" 91 cm	40" 102 cm	44" 112 cm	48" 122 cm	52" 132 cm	56" 142 cm	60" 152 cm	64" 162 cm
Total length measured from armpit to hem	23.5" 60 cm	26" 66 cm	27" 69 cm	30.5" 77 cm	30.5" 77 cm	31.5" 80 cm	34" 86 cm	35" 89 cm	37.5" 95 cm
Yardage required (Base, Stripes*)	345, 1180	390, 1440	475, 1585	590, 2000	635, 2160	760, 2380	850, 2820	975, 3000	1090, 3565
Total yardage required	1525	1830	2060	2590	2795	3140	3670	3975	4655
Meters required (Base, Stripes*)	316, 1079	357, 1317	434, 1450	540, 1829	581, 1975	695, 2176	777, 2570	892, 2743	997, 3260
Total meters required	1395	1674	1884	2369	2556	2871	3347	3635	4257

*The stripe yardage above is the amount for all stripes combined. For just one stripe section, you'll need 169 (180, 199, 223, 240) (265, 282, 300, 325) yds [155 (165, 182, 204, 220) (242, 257, 275, 297) m].

This chart shows the finished garment measurements. This dress is made of rectangle panels sewn together to make the body. This means that the dress measures the same at every point—chest, waist, hips, etc. To get the perfect fit for you, you'll want to choose the size that is closest to or slightly larger than the widest measurement on your body. For reference, the model is 5 feet, 4 inches (163 cm) tall with a 36-inch (91-cm) bust, 27-inch (69-cm) waist and 36-inch (91-cm) hip measurements, and is wearing a size 2. If between sizes, size up, or refer to the Customized Sizing to get the perfect fit. Pattern sizes are written as 1 (2, 3, 4, 5) (6, 7, 8, 9). These sizes align with XS–5XL in the United States.

Abbreviations in US Crochet Terms

ch: chain
dc: double crochet
sc: single crochet
slst: slip stitch
st/sts: stitch/stitches

Customized Sizing

The Gelato Sundress consists of two panels: one for the front and one for the back. If you'd like to make your dress slightly wider/narrower, simply add or subtract dc to your initial starting chain according to gauge. For example, if you want to add 2 inches (5 cm) in width (7 dc) to your widest point measurement, you'd need to add 1 inch (2.5 cm) in width to each body panel, which would be an extra 3 dc for one panel and 4 dc for the other.

For length, you can follow the instructions for the size that corresponds to the length you want. For example, if you're making size 2 but want a 30.5-inch (77-cm) long dress instead, complete the row counts for the size that will achieve your desired length.

Body Panels (make two)

Beginning Section

With your base color yarn, ch 57 (61, 67, 75, 81) (89, 95, 101, 109).

Row 1: Dc in third ch from hook (skipped chs count as a st), dc in each ch to end of row. You should now have 56 (60, 66, 74, 80) (88, 94, 100, 108) sts.

Row 2: Ch 2 (counts as a dc here and throughout), turn, dc in each st across.

Repeat row 2 until you have 10 (10, 12, 13, 13) (15, 15, 17, 17) rows and change to your first stripe color.

Stripe Sections

The stripes are worked in the griddle stitch. This is an alternating pattern of sc in one st and dc in the next st. All following rows are worked where the sc is always worked into the dc from the previous row and the dc is always worked into the sc from the previous row. If you customized your size and added an odd number of stitches to your dress panel, you might end a row on a different stitch than as written here, and that's okay. The important part of this stitch is to work the stitches into the opposing stitch. Pay attention to what your last stitch is in a row, and start the next row with the other stitch. See page 140 for more explanation on the griddle stitch.

Stripe Row 1: With your new stripe color, ch 1 and turn. [Sc in next st, dc in next st] to end of row.

Stripe Rows 2–6: Ch 1, turn, [sc in dc st, dc in sc st] to end of row.

After your last row, change back to your base color. With the base color, ch 2 and dc in each st across (photo A).

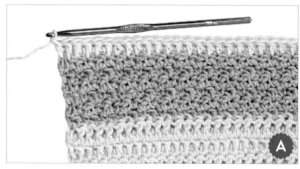

Congrats! You've finished your first stripe section: 6 rows of griddle stitch, then one row of dc. Now, repeat the stripe section 6 (7, 7, 8, 8) (8, 9, 9, 10) more times for a total of 7 (8, 8, 9, 9) (9, 10, 10, 11) stripe sections after your beginning section (photos B and C). Each stripe section (including the row of dc) should measure about 2.5 inches (6 cm).

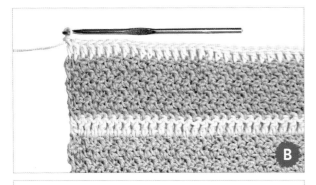

Fasten off after your last row of dc, then repeat for a second panel. This is the longest step by far, but you can do it!

Shoulder Straps (make four)

Using your base color, ch 61. Sc in the 2nd ch from the hook, then sc in each ch to end of row.

Next, place 3 more sc in the last ch (photo D). Then, turn your work so the row of sc is upside down, and sc into each foundation ch all the way down (photo E).

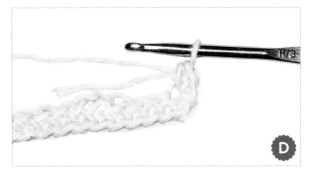

After you've finished, place 2 more sc in the final foundation ch (photo F), then slst into the first sc you made. Cut your yarn and pull through the loop, leaving an 8-inch (20-cm) tail for sewing the straps on later (photo G). Repeat for the other three straps.

Assembly

I recommend the Whip Stitch Method (page 137) for all seaming. Make sure you always seam with the wrong sides facing out.

Sewing the Sides

Working from the top down, seam the sides of your dress together beginning with the base color yarn, as seen in photos H and I. You can switch sewing yarn colors to match the section you're sewing as you go along for an invisible seam. Repeat on the other side.

Shoulder Strap Placement

Before you place the straps, attach your yarn at any point to the top of the body (the foundation chain from the beginning section) and sc in each st (foundation ch) around, then slst into your first sc, fasten off and weave in the end.

Place a stitch marker in the exact middle of the top of one of your body panels. Measure 4.5 inches (11 cm) out from either side and place two stitch markers in those spots so they're 9 inches (22 cm) apart (photo J). Then, whip stitch the side of one of your shoulder straps onto the body where the outer stitch marker is. Repeat for the other outer stitch marker (photo K), then repeat on the opposite side of the body.

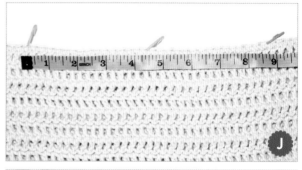

Waist Belt and Top

Try on your dress and place a stitch marker in the dc row where you want your waist belt to be. Mine was in the dc row after my first stripe section.

To create the waist chain that you'll use as a belt, first figure out how long you want it to be. I recommend adding 5–10 inches (12–25 cm) to your own waist measurement.

Using whatever color you like, ch 5 for every inch, or ch 2 for every cm; for example, for a 40-inch (102-cm) belt, ch 200. Slst into every chain, then fasten off. Weave in the ends.

You'll also need a chain for the top of your dress. I recommend adding 5 (12 cm) inches to your chest measurement to figure out its length. Follow the same instructions as you did for the waist.

Waist Belt and Top Placements

To use the waist belt, start from the middle back of your dress in the row of dc that you had marked. Weave the belt over and under each dc all the way around until you finish, then tie in the back.

To use the top belt, start from the middle back of your dress in the top row of dc (the first row of dc you made in each panel). Repeat the weaving process as for the waist belt, then tie in the back (photos L and M).

For a cleaner bottom hem, attach your yarn at any point and sc in each st around, then slst into your first sc. Weave in all your ends, tie your shoulder straps to your liking (photo N), and congratulations! You're done!

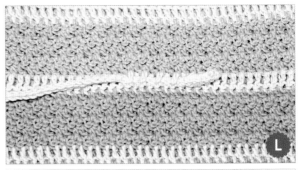

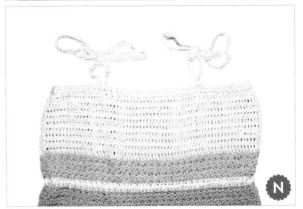

Keeping the Cold Out

As the seasons change and falling leaves are covered by blankets of snow, I'm often tempted to stay curled up by the fireplace. For those times I must go out, though, I make sure to do so in style while staying cozy. The patterns in this chapter are perfect for when you need a simple, warm pullover to complete any comfortable outfit.

Beginners will love both the simplicity and style that the Patchwork Patty Cardigan (page 111) offers. Made entirely of single crochet with a few slip stitches thrown in, this piece is perfect for practicing simple stitches while creating a beautiful end result. The Secret Garden Sweater (page 127) also features patchwork construction, but instead of single crochet patches, it introduces you to the starburst and filled granny squares. You can make this sweater in a million different colors, or just one; the cinched cuffs and hem create a silhouette that complements any palette.

To try your hand at a pattern that only uses two colors, look no further than the Letterman Sweater (page 121) and the Off-the-Grid Sweater (page 103). These pullovers offer crocheters the opportunity to learn new techniques they may have never encountered, including surface crochet, sewing on buttons and making a fold-over collar. For a truly versatile and wearable piece, the Bucur Sweater (page 97) is going to be your best friend. I guarantee you can make several of these sweaters and not get bored; its use of textured stitches and colored stripes ensures a gorgeous garment that makes a terrific gift. These five patterns will ensure that you can do something that is harder than it looks: staying toasty while being in fashion.

Bucur Sweater

Your newest winter wardrobe staple says hello! This oversized unisex design is perfect for anyone and everyone; make it as a heartfelt gift or craft one for yourself in the chilly months. When designing this sweater, I wanted to channel the vibe of happiness. *Bucur* translates to "joy" in Romanian, and this pullover is sure to bring smiles to all who wear it with its simple colors and clean look. The two unique stitches, alpine stitch and griddle stitch, are perfect to add a little bit of texture to the garment and a little bit of knowledge to your crochet repertoire. Pair this sweater with jeans for an easy, laid-back look, or dress it up with a button-up underneath and dress pants.

MATERIALS

Yarn

Worsted weight/size 4 yarn in 4 colors, 1375–2790 total yds (1259–2552 m). See specific yardage amounts for each size in the pattern's size chart on page 99.

Shown In

We Are Knitters Merifine in the following colors:

* ❋ Color 1: Forest Green
* ❋ Color 2: Grey
* ❋ Color 3: Bordeaux
* ❋ Color 4 (and Ribbing): Ochre

Hook

US H/8 (5 mm) or size needed to obtain gauge

Notions

Tapestry needle

Scissors

Stitch markers

Gauge

4 x 4" (10 x 10 cm) = 16 sts and 8 rows in double crochet

4 x 4" (10 x 10 cm) = 16 sts and 14 rows in alpine stitch

4 x 4" (10 x 10 cm) = 14.5 sts and 16 rows in griddle stitch

For double crochet swatch

Ch 21.

Row 1: Dc in 3rd st from hook (skipped sts count as dc) and in each st across, turn. [20 dc]

Rows 2–10: Ch 2 (counts as first dc), dc in each st across, turn.

For alpine stitch swatch
Ch 21.

Row 1: Dc in 3rd st from hook (skipped sts count as dc) and in each st across, turn. [20 dc]

Row 2: Ch 1 (does not count as sc), sc in each st across, turn.

Row 3: Ch 2 (counts as first dc), [fpdc around the dc below the next sc, skip the sc behind your fpdc, dc in next sc] across row, turn.

Row 4: Ch 1, sc in each st to end of row, turn.

Row 5: Ch 2, dc in next sc, [fpdc into dc below next sc this should be the dc between two fpdc from the previous fp row, dc in next sc] across row, turn.

Repeat rows 2–5 until you have 20 rows total.

For more explanation on the alpine stitch, see page 140.

For griddle stitch swatch
Ch 21.

Row 1: Sc in 2nd st from hook, dc in next st. Alternate [sc, dc] in each st across, turn. [20 sts]

Rows 2–20: Ch 1 (does not count as sc), [sc, dc] in each st across, turn.

For more explanation on the griddle stitch, see page 140.

Block your swatches (page 146) if you plan on blocking your garment. Measure the inner 4 inches (10 cm) of your blocked swatches to get the most accurate measurement.

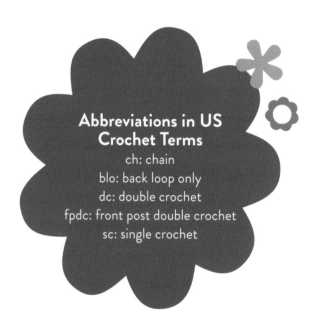

Abbreviations in US Crochet Terms
ch: chain
blo: back loop only
dc: double crochet
fpdc: front post double crochet
sc: single crochet

Bucur Sweater Sizing Chart

	Size 1	Size 2	Size 3	Size 4	Size 5	Size 6	Size 7	Size 8	Size 9
Finished chest circumference	36" 91 cm	40" 102 cm	45" 114 cm	50" 127 cm	54" 137 cm	58" 147 cm	62" 157 cm	66" 168 cm	70" 178 cm
Upper arm circumference	14" 36 cm	16" 41 cm	16" 41 cm	18" 46 cm	18" 46 cm	20" 51 cm	20" 51 cm	22" 56 cm	22" 56 cm
Sleeve length measured from underarm	18" 46 cm	18" 46 cm	18" 46 cm	18" 46 cm	18" 46 cm	15" 38 cm	15" 38 cm	15" 38 cm	15" 38 cm
Total length measured from tops of shoulders	20" 51 cm	20" 51 cm	20" 51 cm	23" 58 cm	23" 58 cm	23" 58 cm	26" 66 cm	26" 66 cm	26" 66 cm
Yardage required (Color 1, Color 2*, Color 3, Color 4, Ribbing)	260, 355, 260, 320, 180	290, 390, 290, 355, 195	315, 425, 315, 390, 210	400, 510, 400, 485, 225	420, 540, 420, 510, 240	420, 555, 420, 515, 270	500, 630, 500, 540, 280	535, 675, 535, 625, 295	560, 705, 560, 655, 310
Total yardage required	1375	1520	1655	2020	2130	2180	2450	2665	2790
Meters required (Color 1, Color 2*, Color 3, Color 4, Ribbing)	238, 325, 238, 293, 165	265, 357, 265, 325, 178	288, 389, 288, 357, 192	366, 466, 366, 444, 206	384, 494, 384, 466, 220	384, 508, 384, 471, 247	457, 575, 457, 494, 256	489, 617, 489, 572, 270	512, 645, 512, 599, 284
Total meters required	1259	1390	1514	1848	1948	1994	2239	2437	2552

*The yardage for color 2 above does not include the yardage used for the neckline/collar. You can use Color 2 as shown in the images, or any other color of your choice! You will need about 50 yards (45 m).

This chart shows the finished garment measurements. This sweater is designed to be worn with up to 8 inches (20 cm) of positive ease, depending on the size you are making. For reference, the model is 6 feet, 4 inches (193 cm) tall with a 50-inch (127-cm) chest and 14-inch (36-cm) upper arm measurements and is wearing a size 5 (4 inches [10 cm] of positive ease). If between sizes, size up, or refer to Customized Sizing to get the perfect fit. Pattern sizes are written as 1 (2, 3, 4, 5) (6, 7, 8, 9). These sizes align with XS–5XL.

Customized Sizing

The Bucur Sweater consists of four panels: two for the body and two for the sleeves. If you'd like to change your sweater's chest circumference, simply add dc to your initial starting chain according to gauge. For example, if you want to add 2 inches (5 cm) in width (8 dc), you'd need to add 1 inch (2.5 cm) in width to each body panel, which would be an extra 4 dc per panel.

The same principle applies to length, though you will want to keep the four sections relatively equal in size. To add around 3 inches (8 cm) in length, add on two rows in sections 1, 2 and 3 and three rows in section 4. To change your upper arm circumference, simply follow the directions for the size you desire for the sleeve panels.

Body Panels (make two)

Section 1

Let's begin! With color 1, ch 73 (79, 91, 101, 109) (117, 125, 133, 141).

Row 1: Dc in third ch from hook (skipped chs count as a st), dc in each ch to end of row. You should now have 72 (78, 90, 100, 108) (116, 124, 132, 140) sts.

Row 2: Ch 2 (counts as a dc here and throughout), turn, dc to end.

Repeat row 2 until you have 9 (9, 9, 11, 11) (11, 13, 13, 13) rows. On your last st of your last row, change to color 2.

Section 2

With color 2, ch 2, turn and begin the alpine stitch (page 140).

Continue in alpine stitch until you have 16 (16, 16, 18, 18) (18, 20, 20, 20) rows in this section. If you don't end on a row of sc, create an extra row of sc. On your last st of your last row, change to color 3.

Section 3

With color 3, ch 2 and dc in each ch to end of row, just as you did for Section 1.

Repeat this row until you have 9 (9, 9, 11, 11) (11, 13, 13, 13) rows in this section. On your last st of your last row, change to color 4.

Section 4

With color 4, ch 1, turn and begin the griddle stitch (page 140). Repeat until you have 16 (16, 16, 19, 19) (19, 21, 21, 21) rows in this section.

Row 6: Ch 1, turn, sc across. Fasten off. Repeat for the second body panel.

Sleeve Panels (make two)

Section 1

With color 1, ch 55 (63, 63, 70, 70) (78, 78, 86, 86).

Repeat row 1 from the body panel section 1. You should now have 54 (62, 62, 69, 69) (77, 77, 85, 85) dc sts.

Repeat row 2 from the body panel section 1 until you have 8 (8, 8, 8, 8) (6, 6, 6, 6) rows. On your last st of your last row, change to color 2.

Section 2

With color 2, work as for section 2 of body until you have 14 (14, 14, 14, 14) (12, 12, 12, 12) rows total in this section. If you don't end on a row of sc, create one extra row of sc. On your last st of your last row, change to color 3.

Section 3

With color 3, work as for section 3 of body until you have 8 (8, 8, 8, 8) (6, 6, 6, 6) rows in this section. On your last st of your last row, change to color 4.

Section 4

With color 4, work as for Section 4 of body until you have 13 (13, 13, 13, 13) (10, 10, 10, 10) rows in this section.

Work row 6 as for body, creating 1 row of sc, and fasten off. Repeat for the second sleeve.

Ribbing

Body Ribbing

In ribbing color, ch 16.

Row 1: Sc in 2nd ch from hook, then sc in each ch to end of row. You should now have 15 sc.

Row 2: Ch 1, turn, sc blo in each st across.

Repeat row 2 until your ribbing is as long as the garment's finished chest circumference unstretched. You can shorten the band to get a cinched-in effect at the hem by removing 5–10 inches (13–25 cm) from the finished ribbing length. Fasten off.

Cuff Ribbing

In ribbing color, ch 16.

Row 1: Repeat row 1 of body ribbing.

Row 2: Repeat row 2 of body ribbing.

Repeat row 2 until your ribbing is 8 (8, 8, 8, 8) (10, 10, 10, 10)" [20 (20, 20, 20, 20) (25, 25, 25, 25) cm] long. This will give your sleeve cuffs a cinched-in effect. Lengthen the ribbing if you don't want a cinched-in effect by making it the same length as the garment's upper arm circumference. Fasten off.

Assembly

I recommend the Whip Stitch Method (page 137) for all seaming. Make sure you always seam with the wrong sides facing out.

Neck Shaping

Place a stitch marker in the exact middle of the top of one of your body panels. Measure 4.5 inches (11 cm) out from either side and place two stitch markers in those spots so they're 9 inches (22 cm) apart, as seen in photo A.

Align the top of your other body panel to the top of this one. Attach your yarn to the outer edge of the top row of one of your body panels. Seam the two panels together until you hit a stitch marker and fasten off. Repeat on the other side of the panel. These are your shoulder seams (photo B).

To finish off the neck, attach your yarn (I used color 2) to any point on the neck opening. Sc around the opening for a total of 4 rounds, then fasten off, as seen in photo C.

Attaching the Sleeves

Place a stitch marker in the exact middle of the top of one of your sleeve panels. Align this stitch marker with the outer edge of one of your shoulder seams, as seen in photo D.

Seam the sleeve onto the body starting from the outer edge of the top of the sleeve panel. Make sure to do this loosely, since you don't want to make the arm seam too tight. The stitch marker should align with the body's shoulder seam as you're going along the length. Fasten off once you're finished. Repeat on the other side.

Finishing the Body

Fold the sweater in half, as seen in photo E. Starting on the outer edge (the bottom row) of the sleeve and using a matching yarn color, seam the sleeve closed going toward the body, then seam down the body going toward the bottom hem. You can switch yarn colors to match the section you're sewing as you go along for an invisible seam. Repeat on the other side.

Attaching the Ribbing

Sleeve cuffs: Attach a 24-inch (61-cm) length of yarn in color 4 to the outer edge of your cuff ribbing. See Sewing on Ribbing (page 138) to learn how to attach ribbing.

Your body ribbing is the same width as the hem of your body. To seam it on, attach your color 4 yarn to your ribbing, then sew it on.

Weave in all ends, and congratulations! You're finished!

Off-the-Grid Sweater

The Off-the-Grid Sweater's classic fit and geometric pattern make it a wearable and comfortable unisex design. The body and sleeves are made of simple rows of double and single crochet, with a vertical slip stitch detailing added on later to complete the grid. This design is perfect for beginners looking to learn a new technique or seasoned crocheters looking for an easy, meditative pattern with pretty details. The construction is very simple, and the crocheting is mindless, so you can find peace in the repetition. Dress it up with a collared button-up underneath and dress pants, or French tuck it into a pair of shorts for a casual look. If you want to practice new techniques while creating a simple grid pattern, the Off-the-Grid Sweater is the perfect fit.

MATERIALS

Yarn

Worsted weight/size 4 yarn in 2 colors, 880–2015 total yds (805–1843 m). See specific yardage amounts for each size in the pattern's size chart on page 105.

Shown In

Lion Brand Pound of Love in the following colors:

* ✳ Color 1: Olive
* ✳ Color 2: Vanilla

Hook

US H/8 (5 mm) or size needed to obtain gauge

Notions

Tapestry needle

Scissors

Stitch markers

Gauge

4 x 4" (10 x 10 cm) = 14.5 sts and 8 rows in double crochet

For swatch

Ch 21.

Row 1: Dc in 3rd st from hook (skipped sts count as dc) and in each st across, turn. [20 dc]

Rows 2–10: Ch 2 (counts as first dc), dc in each st across, turn.

Block your swatch (page 146) if you plan on blocking your garment. Measure the inner 4 inches (10 cm) of your blocked swatch to get the most accurate measurement.

Off-the-Grid Sweater Sizing Chart

	Size 1	Size 2	Size 3	Size 4	Size 5	Size 6	Size 7	Size 8	Size 9
Finished chest circumference	34" 86 cm	38" 96 cm	42" 107 cm	46" 117 cm	50" 127 cm	54" 137 cm	58" 147 cm	62" 157 cm	66" 168 cm
Upper arm circumference	14" 36 cm	16" 41 cm	16" 41 cm	18" 46 cm	18" 46 cm	20" 51 cm	20" 51 cm	22" 56 cm	22" 56 cm
Sleeve length measured from underarm	18" 46 cm	18" 46 cm	18" 46 cm	18" 46 cm	18" 46 cm	15" 38 cm	15" 38 cm	15" 38 cm	15" 38 cm
Total length measured from tops of shoulders	18" 46 cm	18" 46 cm	21" 53 cm	21" 53 cm	21" 53 cm	24" 61 cm	24" 61 cm	27" 69 cm	27" 69 cm
Yardage required (Color 1, Color 2)	780, 100	890, 115	1045, 130	1160, 145	1220, 160	1265, 170	1435, 180	1710, 215	1790, 225
Total yardage required	880	1005	1175	1305	1380	1435	1615	1925	2015
Meters required (Color 1, Color 2)	713, 92	814, 105	956, 119	1061, 133	1116, 146	1157, 156	1312, 165	1564, 197	1637, 206
Total meters required	805	919	1075	1194	1262	1313	1477	1761	1843

This chart shows the finished garment measurements. This sweater is designed to be worn with up to 4 inches (10 cm) of positive ease, depending on the size you are making. For reference, the model is 5 feet, 4 inches (163 cm) tall with a 56-inch (142-cm) chest, 59-inch (150-cm) waist and 19-inch (48-cm) upper arm measurements and is wearing a size 8—there is 6 inches (15 cm) of positive ease at the chest and 3 inches (8 cm) of positive ease at the waist. If between sizes, size up, or refer to Customized Sizing to get the perfect fit. Pattern sizes are written as 1 (2, 3, 4, 5) (6, 7, 8, 9). These sizes align with XS–5XL in the United States.

Abbreviations in US Crochet Terms

ch: chain
dc: double crochet
sc: single crochet
slst/s: slip stitch/slip stitches

Customized Sizing

The Off-the-Grid Sweater consists of four panels: two for the body, and two for the sleeves. If you'd like to change your sweater's chest circumference, simply add dc to your initial starting chain according to gauge. For example, if you want to add 2.5 inches (6 cm) in width (9 dc) to your widest point measurement, you'd need to add 1.25 inches (3 cm) in width to each body panel, which would be an extra 4 dc on one panel and 5 dc on the other panel.

For length, you can follow the instructions for the size that corresponds to the length you want; for example, if you're making size 1 but want a sweater that measures 21 inches (51 cm) long, complete 49 rows instead of 42 for both body panels.

To change your upper arm circumference, you can follow the directions for the size you want for the sleeve panels.

Body Panels (make two)

Let's begin! With color 1, ch 62 (70, 77, 85, 92) (99, 106, 114, 121).

Row 1: Dc in third ch from hook (skipped chs count as a st), then dc in each ch to end of row. You should now have 61 (69, 76, 84, 91) (98, 105, 113, 120) sts.

Row 2: Ch 2 (counts as a dc here and throughout), turn, dc in each st across.

Repeat row 2 until you have 6 dc rows. On your last st of your last row, change to color 2.

Row 7: Using color 2, ch 1 (does not count as a st), turn, sc in each st across. On the last st of this row, change back to color 1 (photo A).

Using color 1, work [row 2 for 6 dc rows, then row 7 for 1 sc row] 5 (5, 6, 6, 6) (7, 7, 8, 8) more times until you have 42 (42, 49, 49, 49) (56, 56, 63, 63) rows total. Fasten off.

Repeat for the second body panel. However, on your second panel, do not do the final row of sc; instead, fasten off on your final row of dc.

Sleeve Panels (make two)

With color 1, ch 51 (59, 59, 66, 66) (73, 73, 80, 80).

Work rows 1–7 as for the body panels. You should now have 50 (58, 58, 65, 65) (72, 72, 79, 79) sts.

Work [row 2 for 6 dc rows, then row 7 for 1 sc row] 5 (5, 5, 5, 5) (4, 4, 4, 4) more times until you have 42 (42, 42, 42, 42) (35, 35, 35, 35) rows total (photo B). Fasten off. Repeat for the second sleeve panel.

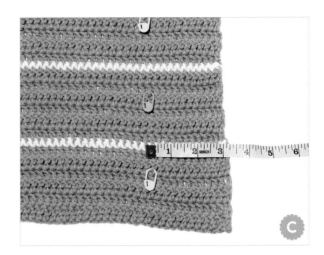

Finishing the Grid

To finish the grid pattern, we're going to do some surface slip stitching, also known as surface crochet. To make it easier if you've never done this before, I recommend doing it first on your smallest panel, likely a sleeve panel.

With color 2, create a slip knot and insert your hook. Measure 3 inches (8 cm) into the side of your panel and place a stitch marker on the stitch that is 3 inches (8 cm) in, as seen in photo C; this will be the column of stitches you'll place surface slsts on. To ensure a straight line, you can place stitch markers along the column of stitches you're slip stitching up.

Now, insert your hook into the foundation chain that corresponds to your column of stitches, going from the top of the panel down through to the back (photo D). Pull the yarn from behind the panel through your panel and through the loop, creating your first surface slst (photo E).

Continue to slst vertically in a straight line up the panel by first inserting the hook in the next place you want to slst, then pulling the yarn from behind the panel and through your hook to the surface (photos F and G). Once you get to the top of the panel, fasten off by cutting a 2-inch (5-cm) length of yarn and pulling it through the loop on your hook (photo H).

Repeat this process 3 inches (8 cm) to the left or right of the line you just created, depending on which side you started from, then do so again and again until you've created lines across the entire sweater, finishing the grid as seen in photo I. Repeat on the other sleeve panel. You can either repeat for the two body panels separately, or if you want to make sure your lines are aligned for the body panels, you can complete it after neck shaping like I did. This can feel time-consuming, but it's worth it!

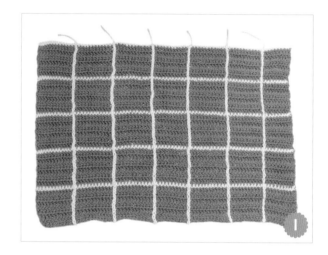

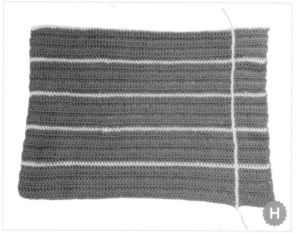

Assembly

I recommend the Whip Stitch Method (page 137) for all seaming. Make sure you always seam with the wrong sides facing out.

Neck Shaping

Place a stitch marker in the exact middle of the top of one of your body panels. Measure 4.5 inches (11 cm) out from either side and place two stitch markers in those spots so they're 9 inches (22 cm) apart, as seen in photo J.

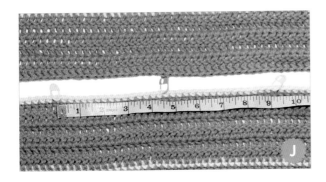

Align the top of your other body panel to the top of this one. Attach your yarn (either color 1 or 2 works) to the outer edge of the top row of one of your body panels. Sew the two panels together until you hit a stitch marker and fasten off. Repeat on the other side of the panel. These are your shoulder seams (photo K).

If you didn't finish the grid on the body panels before, you'll want to do so now. It'll be tedious, but it's worth it!

To finish off the neck, attach color 2 to any point on the neck opening.

For a total of 3 rounds work: Ch 1, sc in each st around the opening, slst to first sc to join. Fasten off (photo L).

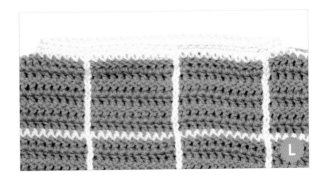

Attaching the Sleeves

Place a stitch marker in the exact middle of the top of one of your sleeve panels. Align this stitch marker with the outer edge of one of your shoulder seams (photo M).

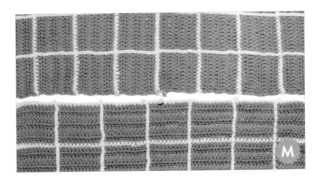

Seam the sleeve onto the body starting from the outer edge of the top of the sleeve panel. Make sure to do this loosely, since you don't want to make the arm seam too tight. The stitch marker should align with the body's shoulder seam as you're going along the length. Fasten off once you're finished. Repeat on the other side.

Final Details

With the wrong side facing out, fold the sweater in half, as seen in photo N. Starting on the outer edge (the bottom row) of the sleeve and using a matching yarn color, sew the sleeve closed going toward the body, then sew down the body going toward the bottom hem. Repeat on the other side.

Attach your yarn to the bottom of your sleeve with color 2. Sc evenly all the way around, then slst into the first sc and fasten off (photo O).

Repeat on the other sleeve. Then do the same on the bottom of the body (photo P). Congratulations—you're done!

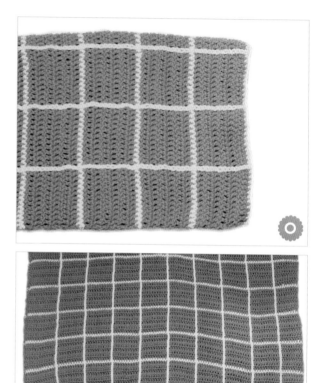

Patchwork Patty Cardigan

The Patchwork Patty Cardigan was the first thing I ever crocheted—I designed it myself, and at some point, while I was making 84 squares, I fell in love with crochet. This design is thus named after my grandmother, Patricia, who always had a dream of being a fashion designer, and whose box full of sewing patterns I admired when I was younger. This simple pattern is perfect for beginners looking to get into garment making. The single crochet squares are ideal: something small, something repetitive, something that lets you practice holding a hook and yarn at the same time. After the stacks of squares build up, you'll assemble them into the final look. This cardigan is a quintessential wardrobe staple.

MATERIALS

Yarn
Worsted weight/size 4 yarn in 4 colors, 1300–2300 total yds (1191–2105 m). See specific yardage amounts for each size in the pattern's size chart on page 113.

Shown In
Hobbii Amigo XL in the following colors:

* ✳ Color 1: Dusty Green
* ✳ Color 2: Dove Blue
* ✳ Color 3: Sand
* ✳ Color 4: Dark Beige

Hook
US H/8 (5 mm) or size needed to obtain gauge

Notions
4 buttons (1.5" [4 cm] each)

Tapestry needle

Scissors

Stitch markers

Gauge
4 x 4" (10 x 10 cm) = 13.5 sts and 13.5 rows in single crochet

For swatch
Ch 21.

Row 1: Sc in 2nd st from hook and in each st across, turn. [20 sc]

Rows 2–20: Ch 1 (does not count as first sc), sc in each st across, turn.

Block your swatch (page 146) if you plan on blocking your garment. Measure the inner 4 inches (10 cm) of your blocked swatch to get the most accurate measurement.

Patchwork Patty Cardigan Sizing Chart

	Size 1	Size 2	Size 3	Size 4	Size 5
Total chest circumference	47" 119 cm	52" 132 cm	57" 145 cm	62" 157 cm	67" 170 cm
Sleeve length measured from underarm	15" 38 cm	16" 41 cm	17" 43 cm	18" 46 cm	19" 48 cm
Sleeve circumference	13" 33 cm	14" 36 cm	16" 41 cm	18" 46 cm	20" 51 cm
Shoulder to hem	20" 51 cm	20" 51 cm	22.5" 57 cm	25" 64 cm	25" 64 cm
Yardage needed* (Color 1, Color 2, Color 3, Color 4, Ribbing)	250, 250, 250, 250, 300	300, 300, 300, 300, 350	350, 350, 350, 350, 400	400, 400, 400, 400, 450	450, 450, 450, 450, 500
Yardage total	1300	1550	1800	2050	2300
Meters needed* (Color 1, Color 2, Color 3, Color 4, Ribbing)	229, 229, 229, 229, 275	275, 275, 275, 275, 320	320, 320, 320, 320, 366	366, 366, 366, 366, 412	412, 412, 412, 412, 457
Meters total	1191	1420	1646	1876	2105

*The yardage above for each color does not include the yarn used for the collar and button bands. You can use any colors of your choice for these elements! I used color 1 for the collar and color 2 for the button bands, as shown in the images. You will need about 50 yards (45 m) for the collar and about 150 yards (140 m) for the button bands.

This chart shows the finished garment measurements. This sweater is designed to be worn with up to 16 inches (36 cm) of positive ease, depending on the size you are making. For reference, the model is 5 feet, 3 inches (135 cm) tall with a 36-inch (91-cm) chest and 12-inch (30-cm) upper arm and is wearing a size 2 with a finished garment bust measurement of 52 inches (132 cm) with 16 inches (41 cm) of positive ease. If between sizes, size up. Pattern sizes are written as 1 (2, 3, 4, 5). These sizes align with XS (M, XL, 3X, 5X) in the United States.

Abbreviations in US Crochet Terms

ch: chain
blo: back loop only
sc: single crochet
slst/s: slip stitch/slip stiches
sk: skip

Color Charts and Construction Explanation

This cardigan is made up of five panels: one back panel, two front panels and two sleeve panels. Each panel is made up of individual squares that you'll sew together later. Figure A shows the sleeve panels, B shows the front panels and C shows the back panel.

There will be 84 squares total for all sizes, and you'll want roughly the same number of squares in each of your colors; for example, if you have four colors, you'd make 21 squares in each color, and so on. This doesn't have to be exact; if you have less or more of one color yarn, you can change the number of squares for that color!

Once you've determined how many squares you'll make of each color, fill out these charts (or sketch out your own!) with a color in each square to reference later. The only rule is not to have two of the same color square touching!

Sleeve Panels

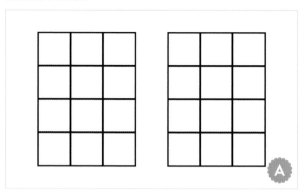

Front Panels

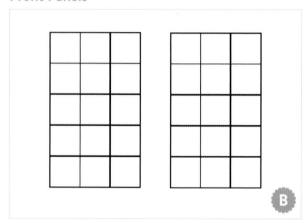

Back Panel

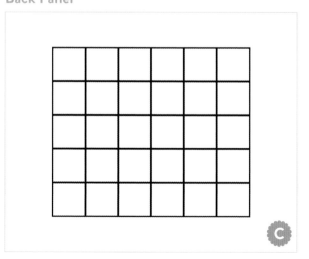

Base Square

Let's begin! Ch 15 (16, 17, 18, 19).

Row 1: Sc into 2nd ch from hook, then sc in each ch to end. You should now have 14 (15, 16, 17, 18) sts.

Row 2: Ch 1 (does not count as a st here and throughout), turn, sc in each st across.

Repeat row 2 until you have 13 (13, 15, 19, 19) rows. Fasten off and repeat until you have 84 squares (all sizes). If your squares don't look perfectly square, that's okay. This is the longest part, but you can do it!

Note: I suggest weaving in the ends as you go along, because the loose ends can become overwhelming if saved till the end.

Ribbing

Body Ribbing

In your ribbing color, ch 10.

Row 1: Sc in 2nd ch from hook and in each ch to end of row. You should now have 9 sts.

Row 2: Ch 1, turn, sc blo in each st across.

Repeat row 2 until your ribbing is 42 (47, 52, 57, 62)" [107 (119, 132, 145, 157) cm] long. You can shorten the band by 5 inches (13 cm) to get more of a cinched-in effect or lengthen it by the same amount to get a looser, more relaxed effect at the hem if you like.

Cuff Ribbing

In your ribbing color, ch 16.

Then, follow instructions as for body ribbing until your ribbing is 8 (8, 8, 10, 10)" [20 (20, 20, 25, 25) cm] long. This will give your sleeve cuffs a cinched-in effect. Lengthen the ribbing by 5–10 inches (13–25 cm) if you don't want a cinched-in effect. Repeat for a second cuff.

Panel Construction

This part will be tedious, but it will be worth it in the end! I recommend the Whip Stitch Method (page 137) for all seaming. Make sure you always seam with the wrong sides facing out. Use a color that corresponds to the squares you're sewing together. For example, if you're sewing squares of color 1 and 2 together, use the yarn of either color 1 or 2. You can attach yarn in different colors as you go to ensure you're always using the right color.

I recommend using a length of yarn twice the length of whatever you're sewing together.

When laying your squares out to sew together, make sure they are all facing the same way. They should be wider than they are long for sizes 1, 2 and 3.

Back Panel

Lay all your squares out according to your back panel color chart. Begin by sewing the squares into six columns, then sew the columns together one by one (photos A and B). This will create a panel that is 6 columns of squares wide and 5 rows of squares long, as seen in photo C.

Front Panels

Lay all your squares out according to one of your front panel color charts. Begin by sewing the squares into three columns, then sew the columns together one by one. This will create a panel that is 3 columns of squares wide and 5 rows of squares long, as seen in photo D. Repeat for the other front panel.

Sleeve Panels

Lay all your squares out according to one of your sleeve panel color charts. Begin by sewing the squares into three columns, then sew the columns together one by one. This will create a panel that is 3 columns of squares wide and 4 rows of squares long. Repeat for the other sleeve panel.

Note: When sewing together your panels, you will be sewing the side that is four squares long onto the body. The size of this side is the size of your sleeve circumference.

Sizes 3–5 only: Attach your yarn to the top right of one of your panels and sc down the width (3-square side) of the sleeve. [Ch 1, turn, sc in each st across] until you've added x (x, 1, 2, 3)" [x (x, 2.5, 5, 7.5) cm] to your panel; it should now be taller, not wider. This adds extra length to your 4-square side to achieve a larger sleeve circumference.

Final Details

Align the tops of one of your front panels (the shortest side; you decide which side you want!) to one side on the top of your back panel (the longest side), as seen in photo E. Starting on the outer edge of each, sew the panels together until there are seven stitches left open on your front panel, as seen in photo F. Don't do any more stitching; fasten off. Repeat with the other front panel on the other side of the top of your back panel. The seams you just created are your shoulder seams.

Place a stitch marker in the middle of one of the long sides on your sleeve panel. There should be 2 squares on either side of this marker.

Note: While creating this pattern, my original design's sleeve panel had columns 3 squares long, so in photo G, there is only 1.5 squares on either side. After pattern tester feedback, I ensured the sleeve was bigger, so there should be 2 squares on either side since there are 4 squares in a sleeve panel column.

Place another stitch marker on the outer edge of your shoulder seams. Line up the stitch markers, then sew the sleeve onto the body so that the stitch markers are still aligned (photo H).

Repeat on the other side with the other sleeve.

Fold the cardigan in half, as seen in photo I. Starting on the outer edge of one sleeve, sew the sleeve closed going toward the body, then sew down the body going toward the bottom hem. Repeat on the other side.

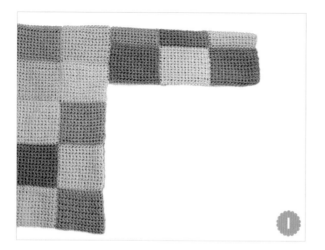

Final Details

Attaching the Ribbing

Sleeve cuffs: Attach a 30-inch (76-cm) length of yarn in color 4 to the outer edge of your cuff ribbing and seam it on. To learn how to attach ribbing to a garment, see Seaming on Ribbing (page 138).

Your body ribbing is 5 inches (13 cm) shorter than your garment's bust. To sew it on, attach a 40-inch (102-cm) length of yarn in color 4 to your ribbing, then seam the ribbing onto the bottom hem starting at the bottom outer edge of one of your front panels; one ribbing stitch will go into one body stitch. If you shortened your ribbing, one ribbing stitch will go into 2 or more body stitches; it's a guess-and-check process, like the Whip Stitch Method (page 137).

Side 1

Row 1: With the cardigan facing you front side up and right side out, attach your yarn (I used color 2) to the bottom front corner of the ribbing of your left front panel, and sc evenly along the side, working 1 sc for every 1 row of sc until you reach the top of the panel (photo J). Ch 1 and turn.

Row 2: Slst into the next 3 stitches, then sc in each st to end. Ch 1 and turn.

Row 3: Sc 4, ch 4, sk 4 sts. *sc 7, ch 4, sk 4 sts* (photo K). Repeat from * to * 3 more times, then sc in each st to last 3 sc. Slst into these 3 sc, then slst into the 3 slsts from the previous row. Ch 1 and turn.

Row 4: Slst into each slst from the previous row, then slst into the next 3 sc. Sc in each st to end. Ch 1 and turn.

Row 5: Sc in each st across to last 3 sc. Slst into these 3 sc, then slst into the 9 slst from the previous row. Ch 1 and turn.

Row 6: Slst in each slst from the previous row, then slst into the next 3 sc. Sc in each st to end. Fasten off (photo L).

Side 2

Row 1: With the cardigan facing you as it did for side 1, attach the yarn you used for side 1 to the bottom front corner of the ribbing of your right front panel and sc evenly along the side working 1 sc for every 1 row of sc until you reach the top of the panel. Ch 1 and turn.

Row 2: Slst into first 3 stitches, then sc in each st to end. Ch 1 and turn.

Row 3: Sc in each st to last 3 sc. Slst into these 3 sc, then slst into the 3 slst from the previous row. Ch 1 and turn.

Rows 4–6: Repeat rows 4–6 from side 1.

Sew your buttons onto side 2, lining them up with the gaps on side 1 (photo M).

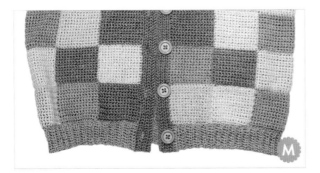

Collar

Attach your yarn (color 1) to the top outer corner of one of your front panels. Sc all the way around the neck opening until you reach the outer corner of the other front panel (photo N). *Ch 1, turn, sc in each st to end*. Repeat from * to * for as many rows as you like to create the collar. I completed 13 rows for a 3.5-inch (9-cm) collar (photo O). Fold it over to achieve the perfect folded collar look!

Weave in all loose ends, and congratulations! You're done!

Letterman Sweater

Unisex, stylish and scholarly, the Letterman Sweater is customizable and comfortable. Inspired by retro letterman jackets, this design can be made in your favorite school's colors to subtly pay homage. Simple, contrasting details serve to bring this sweater to the next level; the striped hem and cuffs draw the eye to the details, while the quarter-button and collar detail give the piece an understated yet sophisticated look. With its full-length body and sleeves, you'll be fully covered from the cold. Pair with jeans for an everyday look for class or work, or don dress pants or a skirt to instantly look put together. A safe foray into color blocking and button sewing, the Letterman Sweater will help you celebrate team spirit while staying stylish.

MATERIALS

Yarn

Worsted weight/size 4 yarn in 2 colors, 1100–2040 total yds (1007–1866 m). See specific yardage amounts for each size in the pattern's size chart on page 122.

Shown In

Lion Brand Touch of Alpaca in the following colors:

* ✳ Color 1: Crimson
* ✳ Color 2: Cream

Hook

US H/8 (5 mm) or size needed to obtain gauge

Notions

Tapestry needle

Scissors

Stitch markers

2–3 buttons

Gauge

4 x 4" (10 x 10 cm) = 16 sts and 8 rows in double crochet

4 x 4" (10 x 10 cm) = 14 sts and 20 rows in single crochet

For double crochet swatch

Ch 21.

Row 1: Dc in 3rd st from hook (skipped sts count as dc) and in each st across, turn. [20 dc]

Rows 2–10: Ch 2 (counts as first dc), dc in each st across, turn.

For single crochet swatch

Ch 21.

Row 1: Sc in 2nd st from hook and in each st across, turn. [20 sc]

Rows 2–20: Ch 1 (does not count as first sc), sc in each st across, turn.

Block your swatches (page 146) if you plan on blocking your garment. Measure the inner 4 inches (10 cm) of your blocked swatch to get the most accurate measurement.

Letterman Sweater Sizing Chart

	Size 1	Size 2	Size 3	Size 4	Size 5	Size 6	Size 7	Size 8	Size 9
Finished chest circumference	34" 86 cm	38" 97 cm	43" 109 cm	47" 119 cm	52" 132 cm	55" 140 cm	60" 152 cm	64" 163 cm	68" 170 cm
Upper arm circumference	12" 30 cm	12" 30 cm	12" 30 cm	14" 36 cm	16" 41 cm	18" 46 cm	20" 51 cm	20" 51 cm	20" 51 cm
Sleeve length measured from underarm	18" 46 cm	18" 46 cm	18" 46 cm	18" 46 cm	17" 43 cm	16" 41 cm	15" 38 cm	14" 36 cm	13" 33 cm
Total length measured from tops of shoulders	22" 56 cm	22" 56 cm	22" 56 cm	24" 61 cm	24" 61 cm	24" 61 cm	26" 66 cm	26" 66 cm	26" 66 cm
Yardage required (Color 1, Color 2)	650, 450	725, 450	825, 450	970, 525	1080, 570	1145, 600	1340, 625	1435, 585	1500, 540
Total yardage required	1100	1175	1275	1495	1650	1745	1960	2020	2040
Meters required (Color 1, Color 2)	595, 412	663, 412	755, 412	887, 480	988, 522	1047, 549	1226, 572	1313, 535	1372, 494
Total meters required	1007	1075	1167	1367	1510	1596	1798	1848	1866

This chart shows the finished garment measurements. This sweater is designed to be worn with up to 6 inches (15 cm) of positive ease, depending on the size you are making. For reference, the model is 5 feet, 7 inches (170 cm) tall with a 32-inch (81-cm) chest and is wearing a size 1 (with 2 inches [5 cm] of positive ease). If between sizes, size up, or refer to Customized Sizing to get the perfect fit. Pattern sizes are written as 1 (2, 3, 4, 5) (6, 7, 8, 9). These sizes align with XS–5XL in the United States.

Customized Sizing

The Letterman Sweater consists of four panels: two for the body and two for the sleeves. If you'd like to increase your sweater's chest circumference, add stitches to your foundation chain according to gauge. For example, if you want to add 2 inches (5 cm) in width (8 dc), you'd need to add 1 inch (2.5 cm) in width to each body panel, which would be an extra 4 dc per panel. The same applies to changing the upper arm circumference.

The same principle applies to length. To add 2 inches (5 cm) in length, add on four rows to each body panel. For the front panel, complete these rows before you start the separated sections.

Back Panel

Let's begin! With color 1, ch 66 (74, 84, 91, 101) (107, 116, 124, 131).

Row 1: Dc in third ch from hook (skipped chs count as a st), then dc in each ch to end of row. You should now have 65 (73, 83, 90, 100) (106, 115, 123, 130) sts.

Row 2: Ch 2 (counts as a dc here and throughout), turn, dc in each st across.

Repeat row 2 until you have 40 (40, 40, 44, 44) (44, 48, 48, 48) rows. Fasten off.

Front Panel

With color 1, ch 66 (74, 84, 91, 101) (107, 116, 124, 130).

Repeat row 1 as for the back panel. You should now have 65 (73, 83, 90, 100) (106, 115, 123, 129) sts.

Repeat row 2 as for the back panel until you have 30 (30, 30, 32, 32) (32, 34, 34, 34) rows. Do not fasten off.

The separated sections

These sections are worked directly onto what you've already worked for the front panel. You'll work two separate sections to create a gap in the middle front where the button band will go.

Row 1: Ch 2 and turn. Dc in next 31 (34, 39, 42, 47) (50, 55, 59, 62) sts.

Row 2: Ch 2 and turn. Dc in each st across.

Repeat row 2 until you have 10 (10, 10, 12, 12) (12, 14, 14, 14) rows. After your last row, fasten off (photo A). Attach your yarn to the other side of your front panel and repeat. Fasten off.

Sleeves (make two)

With color 2, ch 47 (47, 47, 55, 63) (70, 78, 78, 78).

Repeat row 1 as for the back panel. You now have 46 (46, 46, 54, 62) (69, 77, 77, 77) sts.

Repeat row 2 as for the back panel until you have 36 (36, 36, 36, 34) (32, 30, 28, 26) rows. Fasten off.

Assembly

I recommend the Whip Stitch Method (page 137) for all seaming. Make sure you always seam with the wrong sides facing out.

Place a stitch marker in the exact middle of the top of one of your body panels. Measure 4.5 inches (11.5 cm) out from either side and place two stitch markers in those spots so they're 9 inches (23 cm) apart, as seen in photo B.

Align the top of your other body panel to the top of this one. Attach color 1 to the outer edge of the top row of one of your body panels. Seam the two panels together until you hit a stitch marker and fasten off. Repeat on the other side. These are your shoulder seams (photo C).

Place a stitch marker in the exact middle of the top of one of your sleeve panels. On the outer edge of your top, place a stitch marker on a shoulder seam. Lay all panels flat, then line up the stitch markers, then seam the sleeve onto the body so that the stitch markers are still aligned. Repeat on the other side.

Fold the sweater in half so that the body panels are on top of each other and the sleeve panels are folded in half. Starting on the outer corner of the sleeve, seam the sleeve closed going toward the body, then down the body toward the hem. Repeat on the other side.

Final Details

Button Bands

On the top inner corner of your front panel (the corner of the separated section), attach color 2. Sc evenly down the front, then ch 1 and turn. Create 5 rows of sc, and fasten off, leaving a tail of yarn 6 inches (15 cm) long to seam later (photo D).

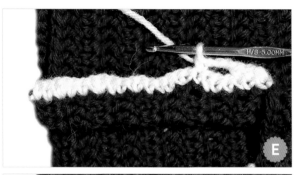

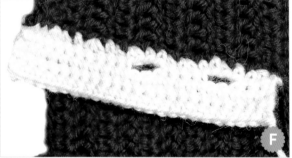

On the other top corner, attach color 2.

Row 1: Sc evenly down the front, then ch 1 and turn.

Row 2: Sc in each st across, then ch 1 and turn.

Row 3: *Sc 4, ch 3, sk 3 sts* (photo E). Repeat from * to * one more time for sizes 1–6 and two more times for sizes 7–9, then sc in each st to end. This creates two button gaps for sizes 1–6 and three for sizes 7–9. Ch 1, turn.

Rows 4–5: Complete two more rows of sc working 3 sc in each ch–3 sp, and fasten off, leaving a tail of yarn 6 inches (15 cm) long for seaming (photo F).

There should be open stitches in between your separated sections where you haven't crocheted or sewn anything into yet. With the right side facing out, seam the bottom of the button band without gaps to the back loops of these stitches. Seam the bottom of the button band with gaps to the front loops of these stitches (photo G).

Collar

With color 2, attach your yarn to the top outer edge of one of your button bands. Sc all the way around the neck opening until you reach the outer edge of the other button band (photo H). *Ch 1, turn, sc in each st across*. Repeat from * to * for as many rows as you like to create the collar. I did 10 rows. Fold it over to achieve the perfect folded collar look, as seen in photo I.

Striped Hems

Rounds 1–2: With color 1, attach your yarn to the edge of one of your cuffs. Ch 1, sc in each st around for 2 rounds, then slst with color 2 and ch 1.

Rounds 3–4: With color 2, sc in each st around, then slst with color 1 and ch 1.

Rounds 5–6: With color 1, sc in each st around, then slst with color 2 and ch 1.

Rounds 7–8: With color 2, sc in each st around, then slst with color 1 and ch 1.

Rounds 9–10: With color 1, sc in each st around, then fasten off (photo J).

Repeat for the other sleeve. Repeat the same process on the bottom hem of the body, but start with color 2 and complete instructions for rows 3–10.

Sew your buttons onto the button band without the gap, lining them up with the gaps on the other band, as seen in photo K. Weave in all loose ends, and congratulations! You're done!

Secret Garden Sweater

What better way to fulfill your patchwork dreams than by making a sweater with two different kinds of squares? The Secret Garden Sweater is cropped, colorful and calming in its construction. I designed this sweater with the intent of making it hard to mess up; beginners can practice their crocheting while making squares, then learn a little about garment construction while becoming their own assembly line to finish the sweater. All crocheters, regardless of skill level, will find joy in exploring this pattern's infinite color combo possibilities while also being flattered by the cinched waist and cuffs. Here's a secret: This cropped sweater pairs fabulously with high-waisted shorts for sneaking through a flower patch into a forest, or with your favorite pair of jeans for laid-back lounging.

MATERIALS

Yarn

Worsted weight/size 4 yarn in 4 colors, 940–2175 total yds (862–1991 m). See specific yardage amounts for each size in the pattern's size chart on page 129.

Shown In

Hobbii Amigo XL in the following colors:

* ✳ Color 1: Light Lilac
* ✳ Color 2: Ecru
* ✳ Color 3: Dusty Green
* ✳ Color 4: Hunter Green

Hook

US H/8 (5 mm) or size needed to obtain gauge

Notions

Tapestry needle

Scissors

Gauge

4 x 4" (10 x 10 cm) = 15 sts and 7.5 rows in double crochet

For swatch

Ch 21.

Row 1: Dc in 3rd st from hook (skipped sts count as dc) and in each st across, turn. [20 dc]

Rows 2–10: Ch 2 (counts as first dc), dc in each st across, turn.

Block your swatch (page 146) if you plan on blocking your garment. Measure the inner 4 inches (10 cm) of your blocked swatch to get the most accurate measurement.

Secret Garden Sweater Sizing Chart

	Size 1	Size 2	Size 3	Size 4	Size 5
Finished chest circumference	30" 76 cm	40" 102 cm	50" 127 cm	60" 152 cm	70" 178 cm
Total length measured from tops of shoulders	18" 46 cm	18" 46 cm	23" 58 cm	28" 74 cm	28" 74 cm
Sleeve length measured from underarm	18" 46 cm	18" 46 cm	18" 46 cm	13" 33 cm	13" 33 cm
Upper arm circumference	15" 38 cm	15" 38 cm	15" 38 cm	20" 51 cm	20" 51 cm
Wrist circumference	8" 20 cm	8" 20 cm	8" 20 cm	10" 25 cm	10" 25 cm
Yardage required (Color 1, Color 2, Color 3, Color 4, Ribbing)	50, 90, 150, 510, 140	65, 115, 175, 610, 160	80, 140, 220, 845, 205	95, 170, 260, 1125, 255	120, 195, 305, 1260, 295
Total yardage required	940	1125	1490	1905	2175
Meters required (Color 1, Color 2, Color 3, Color 4, Ribbing)	46, 83, 138, 467, 128	60, 106, 160, 558, 147	74, 128, 202, 773, 188	87, 156, 238, 1029, 234	110, 179, 279, 1153, 270
Total meters required	862	1031	1365	1744	1991
Number of Starburst Squares you'll make	20	22	30	38	44
Number of Filled Granny Squares you'll make	16	20	28	38	42

This chart shows the finished garment measurements. This sweater is designed to be worn with up to 8 inches (20 cm) of positive ease, depending on the size you are making. For reference, the model is 5 feet, 4 inches (165 cm) tall with a 36" (91 cm) chest and 11" (28 cm) upper arm measurements, and is wearing a size 2 with 4" (10 cm) of positive ease. If between sizes, size up, or refer to Customized Sizing to get the perfect fit. Pattern sizes are written as 1 (2, 3, 4, 5). These sizes align with XS (M, XL, 3X 5X) in the United States.

Customized Sizing

The Secret Garden Sweater consists of four panels: two for the body and two for the sleeves. Since it is a patchwork design, it is a bit more complicated to change the sizing without changing the look, but here are a few suggestions!

For example, for size 2, there are two body panels that are 20 inches (51 cm) wide each for a total chest circumference of 40 inches (102 cm). Since each square is 5 x 5 inches (13 x 13 cm), adding 2 squares to each panel's width to change the chest circumference gets you to the next size up. So, to change the panel width, once you've assembled the panels together, you can add rows of your preferred stitch—sc, hdc (half double crochet), dc and so on—to the sides of the panels to add width before sewing them together. For example, you can add 1 inch (2.5 cm) to each side of both body panels, which would add 2 inches (5 cm) per body panel and thus 4 inches (10 cm) total. Learn how to add length to squares that are already stitched together in Adding Length to Rows of Squares (page 136). You can do the same for the upper arm circumference!

To change the panel length, you can apply the same principles, but add the rows to the top or bottom of your panel instead of to the sides. You can also make the ribbing longer or shorter; across all sizes, the ribbing is 3 inches (8 cm) long.

Base Squares

The recommended squares are the Starburst Granny Square (page 144) and the Filled Granny Square (page 145). You can use any square you like that measures 5 x 5 inches (13 x 13 cm). Refer to the sizing section to see how many squares you're making in total of each kind, and complete that many. This is the longest step, but you can do it!

Ribbing

Body Ribbing

With color 4, ch 15.

Row 1: Sc in 2nd ch from hook (skipped ch does not count as a stitch) and in each ch to end of row. You should now have 14 sts.

Row 2: Ch 1, turn, sc in blo in each st across.

Repeat row 2 until your ribbing is 25 (30, 40, 50, 60)" / 63.5 (76, 102, 127, 152) cm] long unstretched. This will give your waistband a cinched-in effect. You can lengthen the band by 5–10" (13–25 cm) to get a looser, more relaxed effect at the hem if you like.

Cuff Ribbing

Repeat instructions as for body ribbing until your ribbing is 8 (8, 8, 10, 10)" / 20 (20, 20, 25, 25) cm long unstretched. This will give your sleeve cuffs a cinched-in effect. Lengthen the ribbing by 5–10" (13–25 cm) if you don't want a cinched-in effect. Repeat for a second cuff.

Beginning Assembly

In each panel, your squares are stitched into vertical columns, then each column is stitched one by one into a panel. If your column is one starburst square, then one Filled Granny Square, then one starburst, it will be written as so: "Column 1: Star, granny, star."

I recommend the Whip Stitch Method (page 137) for all seaming. I used color 4 for all seaming. Make sure you always seam with the wrong sides facing out. Let's look at how we put it all together!

Body Panels (make two)

For all sizes, the front and back panels are the same, so you'll be doing this twice!

Size 1

* Column 1: Star, granny, star.
* Column 2: Granny, star, granny.
* Column 3: Star, granny, star.

Size 2

* Column 1: Star, granny, star.
* Column 2: Granny, star, granny.
* Column 3: Star, granny, star.
* Column 4: Granny, star, granny.

In photo A, you can see the columns for Size 2 lined up left to right.

Size 3

* Column 1: Star, granny, star, granny.
* Column 2: Granny, star, granny, star.
* Column 3: Star, granny, star, granny.
* Column 4: Granny, star, granny, star.
* Column 5: Star, granny, star, granny.

Size 4

* Column 1: Star, granny, star, granny, star.
* Column 2: Granny, star, granny, star, granny.
* Column 3: Star, granny, star, granny, star.
* Column 4: Granny, star, granny, star, granny.
* Column 5: Star, granny, star, granny, star.
* Column 6: Granny, star, granny, star, granny.

Size 5

* Column 1: Star, granny, star, granny, star.
* Column 2: Granny, star, granny, star, granny.
* Column 3: Star, granny, star, granny, star.
* Column 4: Granny, star, granny, star, granny.
* Column 5: Star, granny, star, granny, star.
* Column 6: Granny, star, granny, star, granny.
* Column 7: Star, granny, star, granny, star.

Now, lay your columns out in order and seam them together one by one into a panel. In photo B, you can see the panel for Size 2 stitched together.

Repeat for a second panel. Congrats, you've completed most of the assembly!

Sleeve Panels (make two)
The same column, layout and stitching rules for the body panels apply to the sleeve panels!

Sizes 1, 2 and 3
Column 1: Star, granny, star.

Column 2: Granny, star, granny.

Column 3: Star, granny, star.

Sizes 4 and 5
Column 1: Star, granny, star, granny.

Column 2: Granny, star, granny, star.

Now, lay your columns out in order and whip stitch them together one by one into a panel. Photo C shows what a sleeve panel will look like for sizes 1, 2 and 3.

Repeat for a second panel!

Assembly

Neck Shaping
Place a stitch marker in the exact middle of the top of one of your body panels. Measure 4 inches (10 cm) out from either side and place two stitch markers in those spots so they're 8 inches (20 cm) apart.

Align the top of your other body panel to the top of this one (photo D).

Using color 4, attach your yarn to the outer edge of the top row of one of your body panels. Seam the two panels together until you hit a stitch marker and fasten off. Repeat on the other side of the panel (photo E). These are your shoulder seams.

To finish off the neckline, you have two options. The simpler one is to create a clean, classic neckline (as shown in the modeled photo). To do this, attach your yarn to any point on the neck opening. Sc around the opening for one round, then slip stitch into your first sc, and fasten off (photo F).

To create a folded turtleneck, work the ribbing instructions as you did for the body ribbing with an initial chain of 25, until your ribbing is 16 inches (41 cm) long. Seam the ribbing onto your neckline. Once the ribbing is fully attached, sew up the ribbing to sew it closed, then double knot the yarn to fasten off. Fold it over to create the perfect folded turtle-neck look! You can sew the ribbing down to the neck opening to make the fold secure if you like.

Attaching the Sleeves

Place a stitch marker in the exact middle of the top of one of your sleeve panels. For sizes 1, 2 and 3, the middle can go on any side of the panel, so the stitch marker will have 1.5 squares on each side. For sizes 4 and 5, this will go on the side of the panel that's 4 squares long, so the stitch marker will have 2 squares on each side. Align this stitch marker with the outer edge of one of your shoulder seams (photo G).

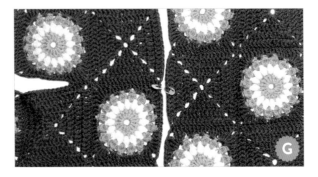

Seam the sleeve onto the body starting from the outer edge of the top of the sleeve panel. Make sure to do this loosely, since you don't want to make the arm seam too tight. The stitch marker should align with the body's shoulder seam as you're going along the length. Fasten off once you're finished (photo H). Repeat on the other side.

Finishing the Body

Fold the sweater in half (photo I). Starting on the outer edge of the sleeve and using a matching yarn color, sew the sleeve closed going toward the body using whip stitch, then sew down the body going toward the bottom hem. Repeat on the other side.

Attaching the Ribbing

Sleeve cuffs: Attach a 30-inch (76-cm) length of yarn in color 4 to the outer edge of your cuff ribbing and seam it on (photo J). To learn how to attach ribbing to a garment, see Seaming on Ribbing (page 138).

Your body ribbing is shorter than your garment's total circumference. To sew it on, attach a 40–80-inch (102–203-cm) length of yarn in color 4 to your ribbing, then seam the ribbing onto the bottom body hem starting at any point (photos K and L). You can repeat the pattern of *1 body stitch into one ribbing stitch, 2 body stitches into one ribbing stitch* from * to * all the way around. This method may need some fussing, but it's worth the trial and error!

Weave in all ends, and congratulations! You're finished!

Crochet Techniques

TIPS FOR CONSTRUCTING AND CUSTOMIZING YOUR GARMENT

Seaming

Almost all of the patterns in this book involve seaming pieces together. You can use any seaming method you like, but I recommend a whip stitch; it is usually the least noticeable, and once you get the hang of it, it's easy and quick to do! Make sure to do all your seaming with the wrong side facing out.

Step 1: If the yarn isn't already attached to one of the pieces you're sewing together, attach it to the outer edge or corner. I recommend using a length of yarn that is around two times the length of what you're sewing together; for example, if you're sewing together 2 squares that are 5 x 5" (13 x 13 cm), use a 10-inch (26-cm) length of yarn.

Step 2: Thread your tapestry needle with a color that matches the section you're going to seam together. You can also use a crochet hook.

Step 3: Insert the needle or hook through corresponding stitches on both panels (photo A). If you're going through the tops of stitches, make sure you're going through both loops on both stitches. If you're going through the sides of stitches, make sure your stitches are even and going through the right stitches—it's easy to mess this up!

Step 4: Next, insert the needle or hook into the next set of corresponding stitches in the same direction you did in Step 3 (photo B).

Repeat Step 4 until you're finished! See photos C and D. I usually double knot my yarn after I've whip stitched all of my stitches together.

For the Starburst and Filled Granny Square (page 145), I attach my yarn in the second chain of a chain-2 space, whip stitch down the side, then finish after I've whip stitched into the first chain of the next chain-2 space.

Adding Length to Rows of Squares

For a few patterns, you'll need to add length to rows of squares, or you can do so to customize your sizing. There are two methods for doing this: One is more convenient, and one is more subtle.

For convenience, after you've stitched together the squares you need to for a row, you can simply add on the extra inches you need with your preferred stitch. To do this, attach your yarn to one corner of an outer square; I do this on the second chain of a chain-2 space. I like to add double crochet, so I chain 2, then double crochet in every st until I hit the other corner of the square. I then chain 2 and turn, then double crochet down the row. I repeat these rows until I've added the length I need (photo E).

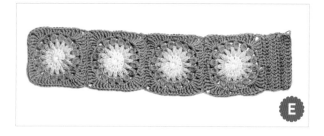

To make the extra inches more subtle and less noticeable, you can add the length to individual squares before joining the squares in a row. For example, if you need to add 4" (10 cm) to a row using this method, you can add 1 inch (2.5 cm) of length to 4 squares using whatever stitch you like, then sew all squares together (photos F and G). Make sure the extra length is horizontal (pointing left or right) when you join them together!

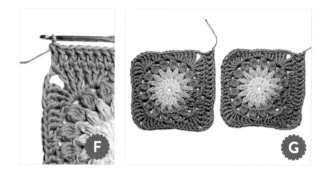

After using either one of these methods, measure the entire row again, including the squares, to ensure it's the right size.

Whip Stitch Method for Panels of Different Lengths

The Whip Stitch Method (not to be confused with the whip stitch) is used to stitch together two rows of squares that are different lengths—for example, a row of 5 squares and a row of 4 squares—that result in one panel with smooth ends. Essentially, you are squishing the longer row to fit the same length as the smaller row. It is mainly a guess-and-check method, but it is very useful for shaping patchwork designs.

Align the two rows you'll be sewing together (photo H). Then, match the beginning and end of both rows and secure them together with stitch markers. Match the center of each strip and secure. Now, you can see how much material needs to get squished to fit in each section.

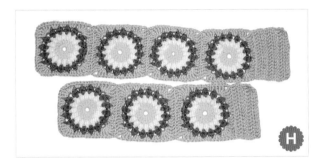

When stitching together, every couple of stitches you will whip stitch 2 of the longer row's stitches into one of the shorter row's stitches. The exact number of stitches you need to do this after is the number of squares in your longer row. For example, if there are 7 squares in your longer row, you would whip stitch together 6 stitches normally, and then stitch two of the longer row's stitches into one of the shorter row's. See photos I and J for examples.

Explained another way: If you have a row of 3 and a row of 4, every 3 stitches there should be two of row 4 that go into row 3. For a row of 5 and 4, every 4 stitches there should be two of row 5 that go into row 4, and so forth. For rows that have a greater difference than one square between them, you'll need to whip stitch two of the longer row's stitches into one of the shorter row's more often, and vice versa.

You don't always have to do it mathematically. If you can match up the rows with stitch markers and just eyeball what you need to do, that works too! It is a guess-and-check method, and you will get more of a feel for it as you practice it more.

Sewing on Ribbing

Similar to the Whip Stitch Method (page 137), you often need to sew on ribbing that is smaller than the garment itself to achieve a cinched-in effect.

To achieve this, instead of whip stitching one ribbing stitch (tip: one ribbing stitch is about one row of sc) to one garment stitch as you would if they were equal lengths, whip stitch two or three garment stitches into every one ribbing stitch. This depends on the width of your garment and the width of your ribbing, so it may take a bit of experimenting to figure out how many garment stitches should go into each ribbing stitch.

Put into practice, it'll look like this: Insert your tapestry needle into one ribbing stitch and its corresponding garment stitch (photo K). After you've sewn that together, insert your hook into the same ribbing stitch, then the next garment stitch (photo L) and sew them together. Insert your hook again into the same ribbing stitch, then the next garment stitch (photo M) and sew them together. Now you've sewn three garment stitches into one ribbing stitch! Repeat this all the way around. Once the ribbing is fully attached, whip stitch up the ribbing to sew it closed (photo N), then double knot the yarn to fasten off (photo O). Weave in the ends (photo P).

If your ribbing and garment widths are the same, simply whip stitch one garment stitch to one ribbing stitch and continue all the way around; then whip stitch up the ribbing to sew it closed and double knot the yarn to fasten off.

Changing Colors

When working the last stitch of your original color, work the stitch as usual, but stop before you close the stitch with the final yarn over and pull through. You'll have two loops on your hook. Then, cut your original color, leaving around a 5-inch (13-cm) tail for weaving in later. With your new color, yarn over and pull through the two loops on your hook (photo Q) and continue your work as usual. I like to double knot the ends of my original color and new color together before I continue my work to make sure they don't slip out.

When working in rounds to create a square, you'll finish the round, then slip stitch with your new color into the first stitch from the round to begin the next round (photo R). I double knot the ends here too.

When working in the round, you'll finish the last stitch in the round, then slip stitch with your new color into the first stitch from the round to begin the next round. I double knot the ends here too.

In this book, color changes only happen when beginning a new round or row, but you can change at any point using these methods; it's a great way to use up scrap yarn.

Sewing Appliques On

To sew appliques on, you'll first need to cut a length of yarn in a matching color; I recommend around 15 inches (38 cm) or longer to be on the safe side. Then, place the applique where you'd like it.

Thread your tapestry needle with the length of yarn. Pull the needle—with the yarn still attached!—through a stitch on your applique, going from the front of the piece through to the back of the fabric you're sewing it onto. This is your first sewing stitch. Then, work your way around the edges of the applique, making small stitches, working from front to back, then back to front. Once you're done, make sure both your working yarn and the tail left from the beginning are on the back of the panel by bringing them to the back with the tapestry needle, then double knot them and weave in the ends.

Weaving in Ends

There are many different techniques for this, but this is how I do it. Before you start weaving, make sure your ends are secure; I make sure mine are double knotted before weaving them in. Always seam on the wrong side as well.

Separate the end of the yarn you're going to weave in so you can see the individual strands that make it up. Depending on the yarn, you may have lots of strands or very few. I usually separate mine into four sections, then weave in each section in a different direction: Up, down, left and right. After I've woven in each one, I cut off any excess, then gently stretch the fabric to hide the ends.

If you want to be a little riskier in hiding your ends, you can simply crochet over them as you go along. For example, while making squares, you can hold the yarn ends together with the piece and complete stitches over them as you go. This is not as secure, but I often use it while making patchwork patterns to keep me sane. You can also do this with whip stitching in ends as you sew two pieces together.

STITCHES

Stitches to Add Texture and Decoration

Griddle Stitch

The basic idea of the griddle stitch is alternating sc and dc, working one st in each st of the previous row. However, starting with row 2, you will always work the sc into a dc stitch and always work a dc into a sc stitch.

Row 1: Sc in first st, dc in next st, [sc in next st, dc in next st] across row (photo S). If you end on a dc, ch 1 and turn. If you end on an sc, ch 2 and turn.

Next, follow one of the options for row 2 below, depending on whether you ended with a ch 1 or ch 2.

Row 2 Option A: If you have a ch 2, this counts as your first dc, sc in the 2nd st, [dc in next sc, sc in next dc] to end of row.

Row 2 Option B: If you have a ch 1, this doesn't count as your first sc, so sc in the first st, [dc in next sc, sc in next dc] to end of row (photo T).

For either option, if you end on a dc, ch 1 and turn. If you end on a sc, ch 2 and turn.

Repeat row 2 until you have the number of rows you need. Remember to always dc on top of a sc and vice versa. This is a great stitch to learn what the back side of your stitches look like.

Alpine Stitch

The basic idea of the alpine stitch is to create texture with alternating front post double crochet (fpdc). Front post double crochet is worked as follows: Yarn over and insert hook around indicated stitch from front to back to front, yarn over, draw up a loop (make sure you are pulling up the loop for your fpdc to the height of your dc on same row), yarn over and draw through 2 loops on the hook, yarn over and draw through remaining 2 loops on the hook. Essentially, instead of working into the top of the stitch that looks like a V, you are working around the post of the stitch itself.

You will alternate rows with both dc and fpdc with a return row of only sc. Each fp row will have a pattern of alternating dc and fpdc stitches that are worked on the previous fp row. But after the establishing rows, you will always be working the fpdc on to a dc from the row below. The result is a 4-row repeat that will stagger the beginning stitches to maintain the pattern.

Row 1: Dc in each st to end of row, turn.

Row 2: Ch 1 (does not count as a st here and throughout), sc in each st to end of row, turn.

Row 3: Ch 2 (counts as your first dc here and throughout; photo U), [fpdc around the dc below the next sc, skip the sc behind your fpdc, dc in next sc] across row, turn (photos V, W, X).

Row 4: Ch 1, sc in each st to end of row, turn.

Row 5: Ch 2, dc in next sc, [fpdc into dc below next sc—this should be the dc between two fpdc from the previous fp row—dc in next sc] across row, turn.

Repeat rows 2–5 until you have the number of rows you need.

Puff Stitch

A puff stitch is made by drawing several loops up in the same stitch and securing them together at the end. Be sure to draw up your loops to the height of the stitches on your row. If the loops are too tight, you won't be able to secure it at the end.

Yarn over, insert hook into stitch, yarn over and draw up a loop (3 loops on hook; photo Y).

Repeat from * to * in same stitch (5 loops on hook).

Repeat from * to * again in same stitch (7 loops on hook; photo Z).

Yarn over and draw through all loops on hook, ch 1 (photo AA). Your puff stitch is complete!

Written another way: [Yarn over, insert hook into st, yarn over and draw up a loop] three times in same stitch. With 7 loops on hook, yarn over and draw through all loops, ch 1.

Repeat until you have the amount of puff sts you need. If beginning a round or row with puff stitch, ch 2 before you start.

Scallop Stitch

Step 1: Attach your yarn and sc in the same st.

Step 2: Skip the next st, then dc 5 into the next st (photos BB and CC).

Step 3: Skip the next st and sc.

Repeat steps 2 and 3 until you have the length you need. If doing this stitch in the round, once you've completed the row, slst into your first sc then fasten off (photo DD).

Written another way: Join yarn, ch 1, sc in first st, [sk 1 st, dc 5 in next st, sk 1 st, sc in next st] to end of row or desired number of times.

Stitch Techniques

Increases

Increases for every stitch are the same. To increase, crochet 2 stitches into 1 stitch. For example:

Dc 18, then inc.

In this, you'll complete 18 dc as normal, then put two dc into the last st (photo EE). This applies to all other st increases as well.

Decreases

Decreases are a little more complicated, and there are different methods for doing them. For example, a dc2tog means to double crochet 2 stitches together. Worked over 2 stitches as: yarn over, insert hook into first st, yarn over and draw up a loop (3 loops on hook), yarn over and draw through 2 loops on hook (2 loops on hook; photo FF), yarn over and insert hook into next stitch, yarn over and draw up a loop (4 loops on hook), yarn over and draw through 2 loops on hook (3 loops on hook; photo GG), yarn over and draw through all 3 loops on hook. Stitch complete (photo HH). You have decreased 2 stitches down to 1 stitch.

The number in a decrease will always indicate how many partial stitches are being created before drawing them altogether. When used as a decrease, it is telling you how many stitches will be used to decrease down to one stitch. You essentially work stitches up until the final yarn over, and instead of completing the stitch, you begin the next one.

Another way to use these stitches is to work them all in the same stitch or space. You are then creating 2 or more partial stitches (collecting loops on the hook) all in the same spot and then drawing through all loops at the end to create one stitch.

A dc4tog all worked into one space in this manner can create a cluster as on the starburst square. It is worked as: Placing all stitches in the same ch-sp, [yarn over, insert hook into space, yarn over and draw up a loop, yarn over and draw through two loops] four times in the same ch-sp. With 5 loops on hook, yarn over and draw through all 5 loops.

Back Loops Only

Back loops only (blo) stitches are typically used to create a ribbing effect. The top of each stitch always has a front and back loop. Typically, you insert your hook under both of these loops when crocheting. The front loop is always the one closest to you when working the stitch and the back loop is always the one farthest from you. If the instructions say "sc blo in each st" then insert your hook only under the back loop to draw up a stitch and complete the sc.

GRANNY SQUARES

This book contains many patchwork designs, some of which require these squares. Make sure each square is 5 x 5 inches (13 x 13 cm). See information on gauge on page 13 if your measurement is different.

Starburst Granny Square

My personal favorite granny square is the starburst. It's just eye-catching enough that it works if you make it in monochrome or with four different colors. Some granny squares can require a lot of color changes, counting or complicated stitches, but the starburst is effortless after you've completed your first two.

The starburst square is typically worked in 4 rounds, with one color for each round. The sample photos are shown with 2 colors, but the instructions are written for patterns that use 4 colors, which is all of the patterns in the book. See page 139 for more details on making color changes. To learn how to dc4tog, see Decreases (page 143). To learn how to complete a puff stitch, see page 141.

With color 1, ch 4, slst into first ch to form a ring.

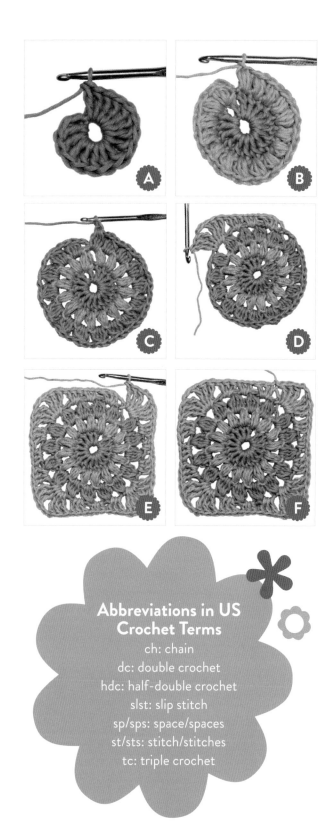

Abbreviations in US Crochet Terms

ch: chain

dc: double crochet

hdc: half-double crochet

slst: slip stitch

sp/sps: space/spaces

st/sts: stitch/stitches

tc: triple crochet

Step 1: Ch 2 (counts as first dc), dc 15 into ring. (16 dc; photo A)

Step 2: With color 2, slst into first dc (the initial ch 2) and ch 2.

Step 3: Complete a puff st in each dc around. (16 puff sts; photo B).

Step 4: After your final ch 1, with color 3, slst into the top of your first puff st and ch 2.

Step 5: (Dc4tog, ch 2) into each ch-1 sp around. (16 dc4tog and 16 ch-2 sp; photo C)

Step 6: After your final ch 2, with color 4, slst into first dc4tog and ch 2 (does not count as dc).

Step 7: *Working into the ch-2 sps around, dc 3 in next sp, hdc 3 in next sp, dc 3 in next sp, (tc 3, ch 2, tc 3) in next sp*. Repeat from * to * around, then slst into your first dc and fasten off. (60 sts and 4 ch-2 sp; photos D, E, F)

Filled Granny Square

This granny square is one that most crocheters will make in their lifetime. I'm a fan because it provides more coverage than the traditional granny square, which is perfect for garments, while still being just as easy as the traditional granny square—all you need to know is ch and dc!

Ch 4, slst into first ch to form a ring.

Round 1: Ch 4 (counts as first dc plus ch 2), *dc 3, ch 2;* repeat from * to * two more times, then dc 2, slst into 2nd ch of initial ch 4 (photos G, H, I).

Round 2: Ch 4 (counts as first dc plus ch 2). Into first ch-2 sp work (dc 2, ch 2, dc 2), *dc into next 3 sts, (dc 2, ch 2, dc 2) into next ch-2 sp;* repeat from * to * two more times, then dc into final 2 sts, slst into 2nd ch of initial ch 4 (photos J, K).

Round 3: Ch 2 (counts as dc in joining st), *dc in each st to ch-2 sp, (dc 2, ch 2, dc 2) in ch-2 sp; rep from *around, dc in each st to end, slst in top of beginning ch-2 (photos L, M).

Repeat round 3, then fasten off (photo N).

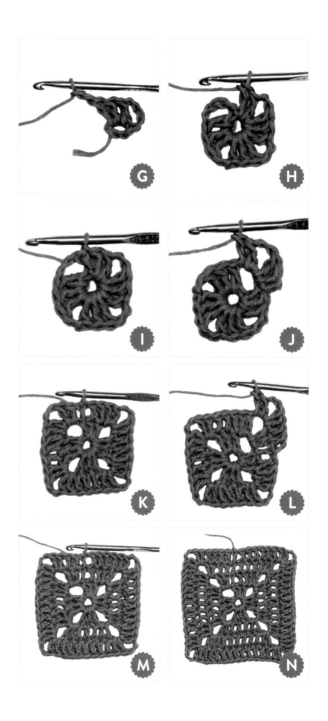

AFTER YOU FINISH

Blocking

Blocking is the process of using water to relax your stitches to even them out, fix any curling edges and achieve proper garment measurements. In knitwear, it's the equivalent of ironing fabric; handmade garments are destined to have a few little kinks, and blocking smooths them out. It is never required during the process of crocheting. I personally have never blocked a garment, but it is an option that many crocheters prefer as it can make your work more professional looking. If you would like to block your garments, here are a few methods.

Steaming: To steam, pin your garment to a blocking board to the correct dimensions, then use a hand steamer to relax the stitches. You'll then let the garment dry fully before removing it from the blocking board, and it's ready to wear!

Wet Blocking: First, you'll soak your garment in lukewarm water with a small amount of mild, gentle detergent or wool wash. Then, use a towel to gently squeeze out excess water, then lay it out on a flat surface to dry. You can also pin it to your blocking board to help keep its shape.

Spraying: As you would with steaming, you pin your garment to a blocking board to the correct dimensions, then spray it with water. You'll then let the garment dry fully before removing it from the blocking board.

With all of these methods, it's important to keep the garments away from direct sunlight while drying, as it can fade the color of certain yarns. You can use a fan to help speed up the drying process if desired.

Acknowledgments

Thank you to my mom, Angela, for telling me everything I make is cute. Your constant support keeps my world going 'round.

Thank you to my dad, Roy, for telling your coworkers about my every accomplishment. I like making you proud.

Thank you to Ray for saying "That's cool!" every time I gain followers. Your truck is my favorite one around.

Thank you to Alex and Rebecca for continuing to enthusiastically receive crocheted gifts. One day, I will have pictures of my own cats in my own house to send photos of to you both.

Thank you to Eden for being the best friend and fellow crocheter a girl could ever ask for. You'll always and forever be my favorite person to do a handshake with.

Thank you to Rose for quick trips to JoAnn's and being the best photographer's assistant. I wish we could be roommates for the rest of our lives.

Thank you to Shelby for understanding my need for gossip and being a gorgeous model. Let me know when you see this so we can play Roblox later.

Thank you to Amangul for telling everyone you know about me and my Instagram. You are my favorite voice of reason when I'm complaining.

Thank you to Adhitya for modeling like your life depends on it. Please continue to respond to my texts asking for medical advice even after you graduate.

Thank you to Leah, Hayden, Grace, Emily and Colby for being the best summer camp friends a girl could ask for. Ok baby forever.

Thank you to Cooper, Ana and Joelle for being my favorite Wellsies, and to the Wells Scholars Program for changing my life. Here's to many more events at Harlos!

Thank you to BK and Aggie for your never-ending support and top-tier purring sounds.

Perhaps most importantly, thank you to my lovely supporters. Without your endless kindness, this book wouldn't exist. Every one of your likes, comments, shares and saves has led to this publication. It means the world to me, and I'll be forever indebted to you for how significantly you've changed my life. To every single one of you—thank you for making me the person I am today, and for your unrelenting support while I wrote this beast.

About the Author

Savannah Price is a fiber artist and designer hailing from Shepherdsville, Kentucky. She picked up a crochet hook for the first time in the summer of 2020 before her first semester of college and never put it down. She created the Instagram account for Savannah's Stitches later that year, and released her first pattern in August 2021. She is a lover of cats, spring flowers, bad reality TV, human rights and sweets. On any given day, you can find her making quesadillas for her loved ones. *Retro Crochet Style* is her first book.

Index